# HOME SKILLS

# Landscaping

## HOW TO USE PLANTS, STRUCTURES & SURFACES TO TRANSFORM YOUR YARD

COOL
SPRINGS
PRESS
*Home and Garden Experts™*

MINNEAPOLIS, MINNESOTA

# CONTENTS

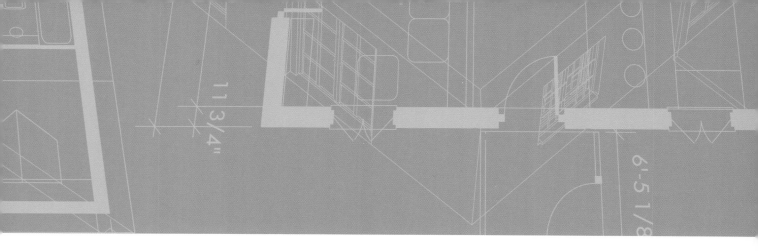

# Building Projects

# Resources

# Introduction

**MOST HOMEOWNERS** already do basic upkeep on their yards, but how about really doing some landscaping? We are all spending a bit more time at home, investing more in our homes than ever before. Our yards present a whole other realm of projects to keep us busy.

The great aspect about landscaping is that there are so many projects you can do yourself with only basic skills and no landscaping background. Most landscaping projects require a little advance planning and a lot of sweat, the perfect combination for a do-it-yourself newbie. And, a huge bonus is that landscaping is very forgiving—you can make mistakes and often no one will be the wiser!

*HomeSkills: Landscaping* has all the information you need to make your first forays into the rewarding activity of beautifying your yard and landscape. *HomeSkills: Landscaping* shows you how to draw a map of your yard to aid in planning and design and what materials are available for your projects. You can use this book to take your yard and make it into the outdoor retreat you deserve. Or, make a high maintenance yard into a low-maintenance dream. Convert a high-water-usage lawn into a low-use landscape. Build walkways and steps to make your yard more accessible and useable and a fence to make it more private or provide a backdrop for plantings.

So let's get started! It's time to dig in and get your hands dirty with some of the easiest, yet most rewarding home improvement projects you can tackle.

# LANDSCAPE DESIGN & MATERIALS

**WHEN IT COMES TO DESIGN AND MATERIALS,** it's a good idea to work things out on paper, when mistakes and miscalculations can be corrected with an eraser and time is the only investment. Mapping out your yard with dimensions and adding structures on paper is invaluable for working up an accurate materials list and estimating costs. Though many landscaping materials are relatively inexpensive, total project costs may become a factor when choosing one style or material over another. This chapter shows you exactly how to create an accurate site map of your yard, including slopes and irregular features. Even if you aren't handy with paper and pencil, you can still create this type of plan. Also covered are the materials you are likely to see when you go to your local lumberyard, stone yard, or garden center and the tools you will need on hand for the projects covered.

# LANDSCAPE DESIGN

Before you dig into the projects in this book, take the time to brainstorm and make a wish list of how you imagine your outdoor space could look. If your goal is to create an outdoor room, consider what elements you'll want to include to accomplish this. Now, get out a scratch pad and begin making some rough drawings of your dream landscape. Think big picture, not project-by-project. Each feature we'll teach you to build complements another project, and you'll find as you build that you want to keep adding more elements to your outdoor space. There's no limit! But, you'll want to take this grand plan in stages, which is why your first task is to create a priority list and start with defining, foundation elements: patios, fences, retaining walls.

Now that you have an idea of how various projects will fit into your overall landscape design, you'll want to focus on the task at hand. While not all landscape projects require a detailed plan, drawings will help you navigate complicated projects with many steps. Here, we'll show you how to survey your yard, draw a site map, sketch bubble plans, draw a landscape design, and create a working drawing you can take to the field—your back yard, that is.

## Tip
**Measuring your yard** doesn't have to be done with precise surveying equipment, but it is very helpful to spend some time with a tape measure before you begin drawing plans. These measurements provide the information you need to create all other landscape drawings. Good measurements are also essential for projects where building permits are required.

Make a rough sketch of your yard, then make measurements that are as accurate as possible. Some landscape projects require digging, so contact your local utility companies to mark the locations of any underground power, gas, or communications lines. If the property boundaries aren't clear, you may also need to contact your county surveyor's office to come and mark the precise boundary lines for you. This can be very important if your landscaping plans will include a fence or garden wall that adjoins the property line.

Straight lines and square corners are easy enough to measure and mark, but it can be a bit harder to

**Measure the position** of all the features of your yard, relative to the property lines. This work may require a helper and a long tape measure.

**Use the survey measurement**s to create a rough drawing of your yard.

precisely locate features that have irregular shapes, or features that are angled in relation to the main property lines. In this case, you can use a method called triangulation to determine precise positions. On a square lot, for example, you can determine the location of a large tree most accurately by measuring the distance to the tree from two corners of the property.

On a yard with significant slopes, make cross-section drawings, called elevations, to indicate the vertical rise of the landscape. Elevations are drawings that show the landscape as viewed from the side. They'll be important for planning fence, garden wall, or retaining wall projects.

Using your survey measurements and the rough sketch,

**Convert all the measurements** you made in the survey to scale measurements. Then outline your yard by drawing the straight boundaries to scale.

**Where you triangulated measurements** from property corners, set a compass to the scale measurements, then draw arcs on the drawing. Where the arcs intersect is the precise location of the triangulated measurements.

you'll now create a more accurate and precise drawing of your yard, called a site map. The site map is an overhead view of your yard, drawn to scale. It is the basis for the finished landscape design. This is nothing more than a drawing that shows the basic permanent features of your yard. It will include the property lines and all buildings on the site, as well as other permanent structures, like driveways or large trees.

A scale of ⅛ inch = 1 foot is a good scale to use for site maps and landscape plans. At this scale, you can map a yard as big as 60 × 80 feet on a standard sheet of paper, or an 80 × 130-foot yard on a 11 × 17-inch sheet of paper. If your yard is bigger than this, you can tape several sheets together.

**Use a plastic triangle and ruler** to mark the edges and corners of all structures within the boundaries of your yard.

## Sketching Bubble Plans

Bubble plans are rough sketches in which you play with different ideas for arranging features within your overall yard. They are a great way to test out different ideas before committing to them. You might, for example, draw your yard with a patio positioned in different locations to see how it feels in relationship to your deck and garden beds.

Draw lots of variations of your ideas, and feel free to play with ideas that seem a little extreme. Professional designers sometimes go through dozens of ideas before settling on one that will eventually turn into a final landscape design.

The place to start is with lots of photocopies of the site map you've created. Or, you can use tracing paper to play with bubble plan ideas. Tracing paper is available at art supply stores.

Make sure to include the other members of your household in this important planning step. They'll be enthusiastic about the work if you've included everyone in the planning process.

**Sketch the landscape** features you're considering on a photocopy or tracing paper copy of your site map. Feel free to experiment; it costs nothing to dream.

**You can test different bubble plans** in your yard by outlining features with stakes and string. You can use cardboard cutouts to represent stepping-stones and walkways.

## Creating a Landscape Design

Once your bubble plan experiments have yielded a plan you like, it's time to turn it into a formal landscape design. The landscape design will serve as a road map for your future landscape. It's particularly helpful if you have a big landscape renovation planned that will take several seasons to complete.

The landscape design can be a chance to have some artistic fun. You can illustrate your design in color, if you want. You may have a few false starts, so it will help to have several copies of your final site map when you begin.

The key to a professional-looking design is to use smooth flowing lines rather than straight lines and sharp angles. Aim for a feeling of continuous flow through the different areas of your landscape. In the final design, the boundaries of the spaces should resemble the rounded flowing lines of your bubble plan.

**On a fresh copy of your site map,** outline the hardscape features, including patio or deck surfaces, fences, walls, hedges, garden areas, and pathways.

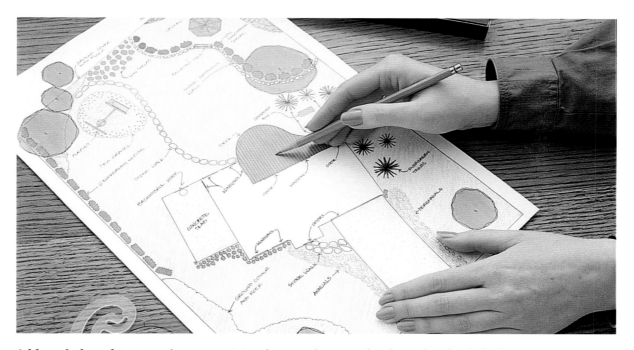

**Add symbols and textures** for any remaining elements, then use colored pencils to finish the design.

## Creating Working Drawings

The final step of this planning process is the starting point for the actual projects you'll find on the pages of this book. Working drawings are individual plans for specific projects within your overall landscape. If you happen to be working from a pre-existing plan, such as a deck or gazebo blueprint, you may not need to make your own drawings. If you're designing your own project, though, making working drawings is what will let you estimate materials and organize your steps.

Working plans serve the same function for landscape construction as blueprints do for builders creating a house. The working plan is a bare-bones version of a plan drawing that includes only the measurements and specifications needed to actually create the project.

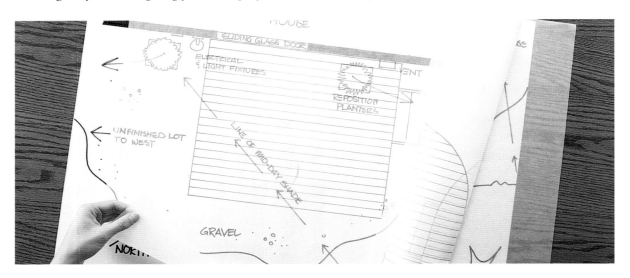

**On an enlargment** of your landscape design, or using tracing paper, make a more detailed overhead view of the specific project, showing structural measurements.

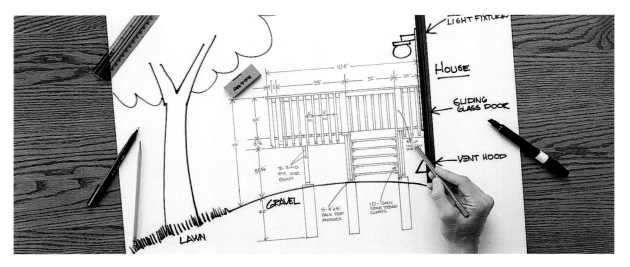

**Create detailed plan** and elevation drawings for your project. List all dimensions on the drawing, and indicate size, type, and quantities of lumber and hardware needed.

## Building Codes and Utilities

Before you can even begin drawing plans for your fence, wall, or gate, you need to research local building codes. Building codes will tell you if a building permit and inspection are needed for a project. Some code requirements are designed to protect public safety, while others help preserve aesthetic standards. For example, in most communities the stringers (horizontal cross pieces) of a picket fence must face inward, toward your house.

Codes may dictate what materials can be used, maximum heights for structures, depths for concrete footings and posts, and setback distance or how far back a fence or wall must be from property lines, streets, or sidewalks. Setback distance is usually 6 to 12 inches and is especially important on a corner lot, since a structure could create a blind corner. A fence or wall may be built directly above a property line if agreed by both neighbors who share ownership of the fence.

If you find a fence, wall, or gate design that appeals to you, but does not meet local ordinances, the municipal authorities may be willing to grant a variance, which allows you to compromise the strict requirements of the code. This normally involves a formal appeal process, approval of neighbors, and perhaps a public hearing.

Another thing to consider as you plan your project is the placement of any utility lines that cross your property. At no cost, utility companies will mark the exact locations and depths of buried lines so you can avoid costly and potentially life-threatening mistakes. In many areas, the law requires that you have this done before digging any holes. Even if not required by law in your area, this step is truly necessary.

A fence, wall, or gate on or near a property line is as much a part of your neighbors' landscapes as your own. As a simple courtesy, notify your neighbors of your plans and even show them sketches; this will help to avoid strained relationships or legal disputes. You may even decide to share labor and expenses, combining resources for the full project or on key features that benefit you both.

**Call 811 before you dig.**
Call Before You Dig will contact your electric, phone, gas, and water utilities, and cable television vendor to send out a representative to mark the exact locations of underground utility lines.

## GREEN LANDSCAPES

As any backyard gardener knows, getting things to grow involves a great deal of trial and error—and also time, money, patience, and even wonder: How can it be that your next-door neighbor has more perfect tomatoes than she knows what to do with when all you can produce is a handful of mealy specimens each year? It could be her soil or her technique, but most likely the difference is that her backyard's microclimate is a better environment for growing tomatoes.

In the bigger picture, this imbalance occurs not just across the globe but also from county to county. Yet, you can visit any garden center in, say, Colorado, and find a huge selection of plants that evolved not on the Western plains but in coastal climates or even the dampest regions of Scotland. These plants may survive in the dry Colorado air with enormous amounts of irrigation and probably lots of chemicals, but it begs the question: Why fight nature?

Choosing plants that are well-adapted to the local climate (and your yard's microclimate) is the first step in creating a green landscape, both literally and figuratively. In many regions, this also means limiting the amount of conventional grass because of its insatiable thirst for water. The next step is to look for ways to use water more efficiently and for collecting free water when Mother Nature provides it.

When it comes to the manufactured elements of the landscape, the basic precepts of green building apply: Choose renewable, recyclable, and healthful materials such as recycled-plastic decking and locally produced mulch. Also consider permeable paving in place of concrete and asphalt to keep storm runoff in the ground instead of loading up the sewer system with water and all the yard and driveway chemicals it brings with it. In this illustration you'll find some of the features in a well-planned, low-maintenance landscape.

### Tip

Don't have a green thumb? Master Gardeners are advanced gardeners who have taken coursework and usually have years of experience in your area. In order to maintain their Master Gardener designation they volunteer at events, community education centers, and Q & A sessions. Find one by asking at your local university extension service.

**A green yard** tends to look very natural and very at-home in its surroundings. It should be populated with native plants that don't require heroic efforts to thrive and it should require little or no watering or chemical fertilization. Ideally, a green yard also has a positive impact on your home and property by providing valuable shade or preventing soil erosion.

# ELEMENTS OF A GREEN YARD

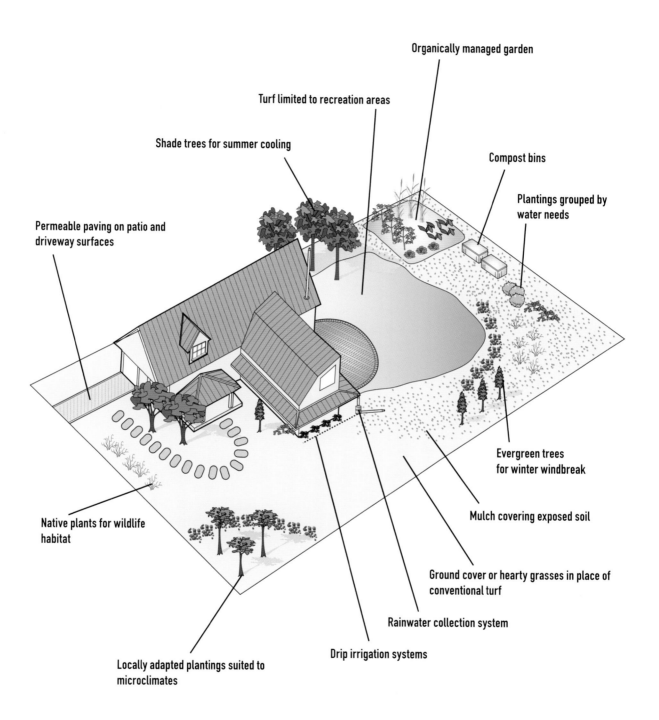

Organically managed garden

Turf limited to recreation areas

Shade trees for summer cooling

Compost bins

Plantings grouped by water needs

Permeable paving on patio and driveway surfaces

Native plants for wildlife habitat

Evergreen trees for winter windbreak

Mulch covering exposed soil

Ground cover or hearty grasses in place of conventional turf

Rainwater collection system

Drip irrigation systems

Locally adapted plantings suited to microclimates

## LANDSCAPE MATERIALS

As with most building projects, choosing the right materials for your landscape is really a question of priorities. What do you value most highly—appearance, durability, ease of maintenance, or cost? Your decision will most likely involve a combination of all of these factors along with a few compromises.

From natural to manufactured, the range of materials available today for landscape projects offers many options. You may choose materials that blend with your existing yard and architectural features, or you may go another direction entirely, such as preferring a brand-new element for your yard because it adds a bit of contrast and panache.

### Wood and Vinyl

Wood is still the most commonly used material for fences and is really the only one that allows for custom designs and details as it is ultimately workable. For outdoor applications your best choices are woods that are naturally rot- and bug-resistant, like cedar, redwood, or cypress, or you can choose pine that has been pressure treated with chemicals to prevent rot. Unfortunately, the pressure treated lumber is not as attractive, but it is much less expensive.

Local climate conditions may also impact your choices. Wood will degrade more quickly in high moisture areas. Under desert conditions, wood may last much longer. If termites are a local problem, then treated lumber or vinyl is a necessity.

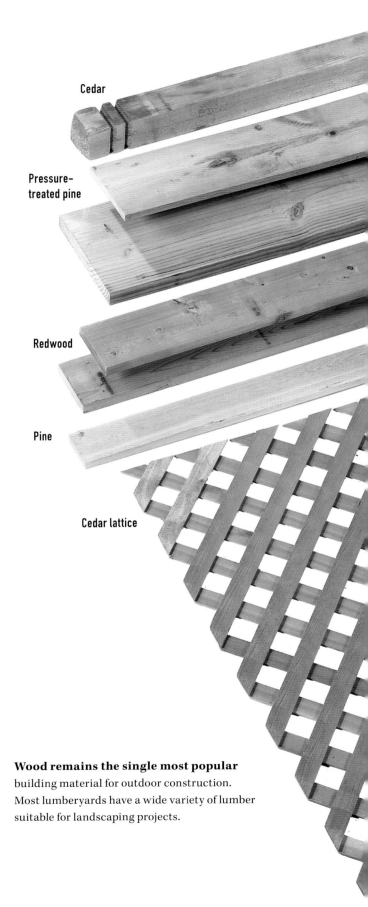

Cedar

Pressure-treated pine

Redwood

Pine

Cedar lattice

> ### Tip
> **Contact with the ground** or moist surfaces speeds the rotting of wood. To avoid ground contact, use concrete footings with metal stand-offs to anchor wood fence posts.

**Wood remains the single most popular** building material for outdoor construction. Most lumberyards have a wide variety of lumber suitable for landscaping projects.

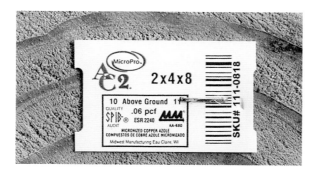

**Pressure-treated lumber stamps** list the type of preservative and the chemical retention level, as well as the exposure rating and the name and location of the treating company.

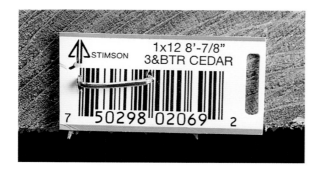

**Cedar grade stamps** list the mill number, moisture content, species, lumber grade, and membership association. Western red cedar (WRC) or incense cedar (INC) for decks should be heartwood (HEART) with a maximum moisture content of 15% (MC15).

**Plastic materials** (right) such as PVC vinyl and fiberglass reinforced plastic (FRP) are generally used in applications such as fencing and lawn edging. Many styles and sizes are available, and they are strong, versatile, and require no maintenance. Some fence materials are sold as kits, making installation easy.

## Stone and Concrete

Natural stone offers beautiful color, interesting texture, and great durability, making it one of the very best building materials for outdoor construction. Although it is more expensive than many other materials, if it fits in your budget, you're not likely to regret choosing stone. It is a good choice for edging, walls, walkways, ponds, fountains, and waterfalls. Natural stone is also used to accent flowers and plants creating depth in garden areas (this is a great way to use stone if you can't afford huge amounts of it).

Each type of stone offers a distinctive look, as well as a specific durability and workability. The nature of your project will often dictate the best form of stone to use. When shopping for stone, describe your project to the supplier and ask him or her to suggest a stone that meets your needs.

Fieldstone, sometimes called river rock, is used to build retaining walls, ornamental garden walls, and rock gardens. When split into smaller pieces, fieldstone can be used in projects with mortar. When cut into small pieces, or quarried stone, fieldstone is called cobblestone, a common material in walks and paths.

Ashlar, or wall stone, is quarried granite, marble, or limestone that has been smooth-cut into large blocks, ideal for creating clean lines with thin mortar joints. Cut stone works well for stone garden walls, but because of its expense, its use is sometimes limited to decorative wall caps.

Flagstone is large slabs of sedimentary rock with naturally flat surfaces. Limestone, sandstone, slate, and shale are the most common types of flagstone. It is usually cut into pieces up to 3 inches thick, for use in walks, steps, and patios. Smaller pieces—less than 16 inches square—are often called steppers.

Rubble is irregular pieces of quarried stone, usually with one split or finished face. It is widely used in wall construction.

**Fieldstone is stone** gathered from fields, dry riverbeds, and hillsides. It is used in wall construction.

**Flagstone consists of large slabs** of quarried stone cut into pieces up to 3" thick. It is used in walks, steps, and patios.

### Tip

A stone yard is a great place to get ideas and see the types of stone that are available. This stone yard includes a display area that identifies different types of stone and suggests ways they can be used.

**Interlocking
wall blocks**

**Molded paver slabs**

**Paver bricks**

**Exposed aggregate
paver slabs**

**Concrete
paver slabs**

Manufactured stone is designed to resemble natural stone, but because it's more uniform it is easier to install and generally costs less. Concrete products are being offered in more styles all the time, giving you a lot of flexibility to build distinctive projects that are also reasonably priced.

Concrete paver slabs, available in several shapes and sizes, are used for laying simple walkways and patios. They're available in a standard finish, a smooth aggregate finish, or can be colored and molded to resemble brick or cobblestone. Concrete paver slabs are relatively inexpensive and quite easy to work with. They're usually laid in a bed of sand and require no mortar. Their surface is sometimes finished so the smooth gravel aggregate is exposed, but they are also available in plain pavers and colored slabs.

Paver bricks resemble traditional kiln-dried clay bricks but are more durable and easier to install. Paver bricks come in many colors and shapes and are ideal for paving patios, walkways, and driveways. Many varieties are available in interlocking shapes that can be combined with standard bricks to create decorative patterns, such as herringbone and basket weave. Edging blocks are precast in different sizes for creating boundaries to planting areas, lawns, loose-fill paths, and retaining walls.

**Tip**

**Veneer stone** is natural or manufactured stone cut or molded for use in nonload-bearing, cosmetic applications, such as facing exterior walls or freestanding concrete block walls.

**Concrete products for landscaping** are available in a wide range of colors, sizes, and shapes.

## Loose Materials

Loose materials for patios and walkways encompass a wide range of natural elements, from gravel to wood chips to small river stones. You can use a loose material by itself to create a simple patio or path surface or use it as infill between an arrangement of heavier materials, such as flagstone or large, concrete stepping pavers. In contrast to the solidity and permanence of traditional paving, loose materials have a casual, summery feel. Walking over a pathway of crushed stone or wood chips can feel like a stroll down a country lane or a walk through the woods. As a primary surface, loose materials offer several practical advantages. They drain well, are forgiving of uneven ground, and can be replenished and graded with a rake for a quick facelift. They also tend to be much less expensive than most other paving options and couldn't be easier to install. In a typical installation, start with a bed of compacted gravel and cover it with landscape fabric to inhibit weed growth and separate the gravel base from the surface material. Then, spread out the surface material a few inches thick, compact it if necessary, and you're done! For simpler applications, such as a lightly traveled garden path, you can often skip the gravel base and lay the landscape fabric right over leveled and tamped soil. In most cases, it's best to include a raised edging of some kind to contain the materials and maintain the shape of the paved surface.

## Selecting Loose Materials

Because different loose materials can have very different textures and properties, it's important to choose the right surface for the application. Here's a look at some of the most popular materials for patios and walkways:

**Decomposed granite**

Decomposed granite: A popular choice for level patios, paths, and driveways, decomposed granite (DG) can be compacted to a relatively smooth, flat, hard surface. DG consists of small pieces of granite ranging in size from sand-size grains to a quarter inch—this size variation is the reason this material is so compactable. DG is available in various natural shades of gray, brown, and tan. Due to its gritty, sandy finish that can stick to your shoes, DG is not a good choice for surfaces that receive heavy traffic directly to and from the house.

**Loose materials can work well** on their own or as a complement to surrounding elements. In this landscape, buff-colored gravel serves as both a primary surface and an infill material for a stepping stone path. The natural look of the gravel provides a nice contrast to the formal paver walkway and patio.

**Crushed stone**

Pea gravel and crushed stone include a broad
range of gravel, from fairly fine textures to very
coarse. Pea gravel is small- to medium-sized rounded
stone. Crushed stone typically consists of coarse,
jagged pieces in various sizes, generally larger than
pea gravel. Many types of gravel are compactable, but
usually less so than DG.

**River Rock**

Smoothed and rounded by water or machines,
river rock ranges from small stones to baseball-sized
(and larger) rocks. These smooth surfaces make it
more comfortable to walk on than jagged gravel but it
is also less compactable and easily displaced
underfoot. Larger stones are difficult to walk on and
are more suitable for infill and accent areas than for
primary paving surfaces.

**Wood chips**

Wood chips and mulch are commonly used as
groundcover in planting beds, gardens, and
flowerbeds. Most types are soft and springy
underfoot, and many can be used for light-traffic
paths and even children's play areas. Wood chips
come in a wide variety of grades, colors, and textures.
In general, finely chopped and consistent materials
are more expensive and more formal in appearance
than coarse blends. The term mulch is often used
interchangeably with wood chips but can also
describe roughly chopped wood and other organic
matter that's best suited for beds and ground cover.
Most loose material made of wood needs some
replenishing every two to four years.

Both stone and wood loose materials are typically
sold in bulk at landscape and garden centers and by
the bag at home centers. Buying in bulk is often much
less expensive for all but the smallest jobs. Landscape
and garden suppliers typically offer bulk deliveries for
a reasonable flat fee. Due to the variance in
terminology and appearance of loose materials, be
sure to visit the supplier and take a look at the
materials you're buying firsthand, so you know
exactly what to expect.

## Concrete & Mortar

Poured concrete is used for driveways, walkways, and patios because of its exceptional strength. Although it is sometimes criticized for its bland appearance, concrete in modern use is often tinted or given a surface finish that lets it simulate brick pavers or flagstone at a fraction of the cost. Concrete can also be formed into curves and other shapes, such as edging, ponds, or fountains. Setting fence posts is the most common use of concrete for do-it-yourself landscapers. Mortar is used for laying brick and mortared stone walls.

**Bagged concrete** mix comes in many formulations. The selection you're likely to encounter varies by region and by time of year, but the basic products most home centers stock include: all-purpose concrete (A, C) for posts, footings, and slabs; sand mix (B) for topping and casting; Portland cement (D) for mixing with aggregate, sand, and water to make your own concrete; high/early concrete (E) for driveways and other projects that demand greater shock and crack resistance; fast-setting concrete (F) for setting posts and making repairs; specialty blends for specific purposes, such as countertop mix (G), which comes premixed with polyester fibers and additives that make it suitable for countertops.

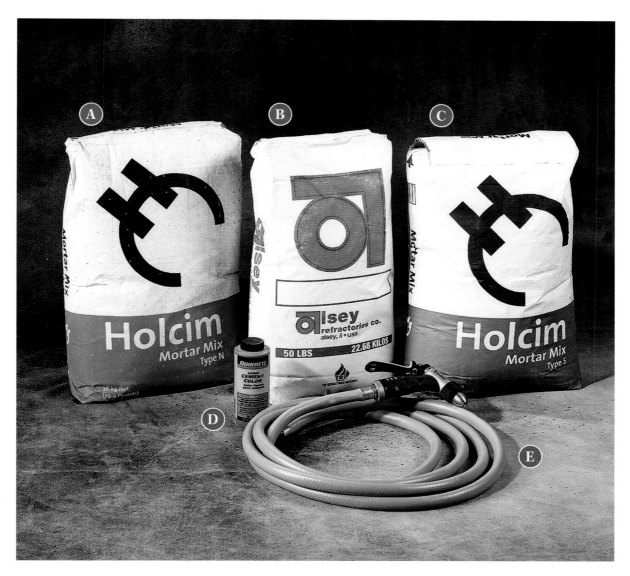

**Mortar Mixes:** Type N, a medium-strength mortar for above-grade outdoor use in nonload-bearing (freestanding) walls, barbeques, chimneys, and tuck-pointing (A); refractory mortar, a calcium aluminate mortar that is resistant to high temperatures, used for mortaring around firebrick in fireplaces and barbeques (B); Type S, a high-strength mortar for outdoor use at or below grade, typically used in foundations, retaining walls, driveways, walks, and patios (C); mortar tint for coloring mortar (D); and you'll need water for mixing mortar so a hose is needed (E) (a sprayer attachment is needed later to clean the surface).

## Hardware & Fasteners

Although they're rarely visible, the metal spikes, screws, nails, bolts, and other hardware items can be crucial to a successful landscaping project.

The chemicals now used in pressure-treated lumber may require metal connectors specially designed to withstand the corrosive effect of these chemicals. Specifically, manufacturers suggest that metal connectors used with pressure-treated lumber be galvanized with a hot-dip process rather than a mechanical zinc plating. Triple-dipped, hot-dipped galvanized fasters are the best.

Cedar, redwood, and cypress will stain if galvanized fasteners are used. If you will be letting the wood weather, or will be using a clear sealer or a light stain, use specially coated hardware or stainless steel fasteners. If you will be painting, the fasteners only need to be corrosion resistant. Stainless can also be used with pressure-treated lumber. The disadvantage of stainless steel is the expense. Do not use aluminum fasteners with pressure-treated lumber.

There are a number of head-driving options available for exterior-rated screws. Square and Torx-drive screws will not slip while fastening like Phillips heads. Posi-drive screws are very popular because they combine Phillips and square-drive heads, giving you a choice of which to use.

## Estimating & Ordering Materials

Even with small projects, it's important to take careful measurements and estimate accurately. Landscaping materials are bulky and are expensive and time consuming to transport, so accurate estimating will save you time and money. Begin compiling a materials list by reviewing the scale drawing of your building plans (pages 10 to 11), then use the information here to estimate materials. Once you have developed a materials list, add 10 percent to the estimate for each item to allow for waste and small oversights.

The cost of your project will depend upon which building materials you choose. You can save money by choosing materials that are readily available in your area. This is particularly true of natural stone products. Choosing stone that is quarried locally is far less expensive than exotic stone transported long distances. Lumber, metal, and plastics can also vary widely in price, depending on where they're milled or manufactured.

Most of what you need is available at large, general-purpose home centers, but for landscaping projects you may want to buy some materials from specialty retailers. A large concrete project, for example, will be cheaper if you buy ready-mix concrete instead of bagged concrete mix from your home center.

If you plan on working with specialty or alternative materials, such as vinyl fencing or composite decking, many home centers will have a select range of styles and sizes on hand but can also order specialty materials for you.

Head styles for exterior screws include: Posi-drive (A), torx (B), square drive (C), and phillips (D).

### Tip

A cordless drill can make landscape projects like fencing move much more quickly. If you are using treated lumber, which is made heavy and wet from the treatment, you will need a more powerful drill/driver than what you need for untreated lumber.

If you are installing landscape timbers, you will need a powerful drill and an extra long drill bit to drill the holes for the spikes.

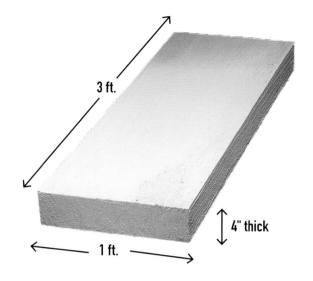

3 ft.

4" thick

1 ft.

**A contractor's calculator** can convert measurements and estimate concrete volume. The calculator isn't very expensive and will relieve you of complex math conversions. It's also handy for estimating fencing materials and paint coverage.

**To estimate concrete volume,** measure the width and length of the project in feet, then multiply the dimensions to get the square footage. Measure the thickness in feet (4" thick equals ⅓ ft.), then multiply the square footage times the thickness to get the cubic footage. For example, 1 ft. × 3 ft. × ⅓ ft. = 1 cu. ft. Twenty-seven cubic feet equals 1 cubic yard.

**Local brick and stone suppliers** will often help you design your project and advise you about estimating materials, local building codes, and climate considerations.

## ESTIMATING MATERIALS

| | |
|---|---|
| Sand, gravel, topsoil (2" layer) | surface area (sq. ft.) ÷ 100 = tons needed |
| Standard brick pavers for walks (2" layer) | surface area (sq. ft.) × 5 = number of pavers needed |
| Standard bricks for walls and pillars (4 × 8") | surface area (sq. ft.) × 7 = number of bricks needed (single-brick thickness) |
| Poured concrete (4" layer) | surface area (sq. ft.) × .012 = cubic yards needed |
| Flagstone | surface area (sq. ft.) ÷ 100 = tons needed |
| Interlocking block (2" layer) | area of wall face (sq. ft.) × 1.5 = number of blocks needed |
| Ashlar stone for 1-ft.-thick walls | area of wall face (sq. ft.) ÷ 15 = tons of stone needed |
| Rubble stone for 1-ft.-thick walls | area of wall face (sq. ft.) ÷ 35 = tons of stone needed |
| 8 × 8 × 16" concrete block for freestanding walls | height of wall (ft.) × length of wall (ft.) × 1.125 = number of blocks needed |

## AMOUNT OF CONCRETE NEEDED (CU. FT.)

| Number of 8"-diameter footings | Depth of footings (ft.) | | | |
|---|---|---|---|---|
| | 1 ft. | 2 ft. | 3 ft. | 4 ft. |
| 2 | ¾ | 1½ | 2¼ | 3 |
| 3 | 1 | 2¼ | 3½ | 4½ |
| 4 | 1½ | 3 | 4½ | 6 |
| 5 | 2 | 3¾ | 5¾ | 7½ |

## CONCRETE COVERAGE

| Volume | Thickness | Surface coverage |
|---|---|---|
| 1 cu. yd. | 2" | 160 sq. ft. |
| 1 cu. yd. | 3" | 110 sq. ft. |
| 1 cu. yd. | 4" | 80 sq. ft. |
| 1 cu. yd. | 5" | 65 sq. ft. |
| 1 cu. yd. | 6" | 55 sq. ft. |
| 1 cu. yd. | 8" | 40 sq. ft. |

## DRY INGREDIENTS FOR SELF-MIX

| Amount of concrete needed (cu. ft.) | 94-lb. bags of portland cement | Cubic feet of sand | Cubic feet of gravel | 60-lb. bags of premixed dry concrete |
|---|---|---|---|---|
| 1 | ⅙ | ⅓ | ½ | 2 |
| 2 | ⅓ | ⅔ | 1 | 4 |
| 3 | ½ | 1 ½ | 3 | 6 |
| 4 | ¾ | 1 ¾ | 3 ½ | 8 |
| 5 | 1 | 2 ¼ | 4 ½ | 10 |
| 10 | 2 | 4 ½ | 9 | 20 |

## TOOLS

The landscaper's tool shed contains a range of basic hand tools, larger specialty tools, masonry tools, and power tools. As you take on projects in this book, you'll gradually expand your everyday tool box to a well-rounded collection that could easily fill a shed. You may not want to purchase every tool, and that's where rental centers come in handy. Many landscape supply and hardware stores also have equipment available for rent. If you'll use the equipment one time, or on a very limited basis, this is the most cost-effective way to acquire the tools you need without investing heavily in equipment that will sit unused 99 percent of the time.

Metal tools should be made from high-carbon steel with smoothly finished surfaces. Hand tools

**Tip**
For tools you decide to purchase, invest in the best you can afford. Estate sales often have good quality tools for less—and if the handle is ruined, replacements are available.

should be well-balanced and have tight, comfortably molded handles. Pick up the tool. How does it feel? Ergonomics are a big deal because you'll be spending lots of time handling your basic tools. Consider the length of the shaft on shovels, landscape rakes, etc. You can find adjustable options that allow you to "size" the equipment to suit your body.

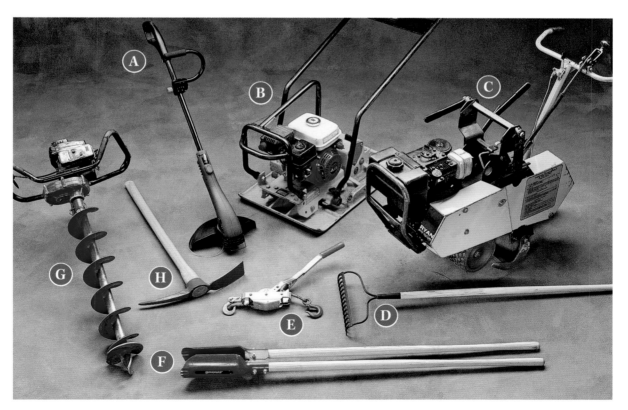

**Specialty tools** for landscape and yard work include: weed trimmer for clearing light brush (A), power tamper for compacting soil and subbase material (B), power sod cutter (C), garden rake or bow rake (D), come-along manual winch to assist in moving heavy objects (E), post-hole digger (F), gas-powered auger (G), pick axe (H).

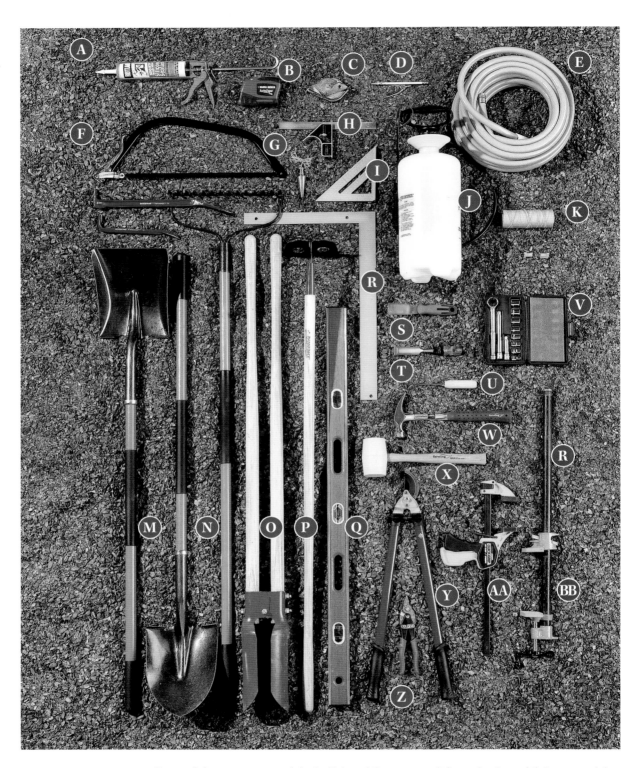

**Hand tools include:** caulk gun (A), tape measure (B), chalk line (C), compass (D), garden hose (E), bow saw (F), plumb bob (G), combination square (H), speed square (I), pressure sprayer (J), mason's line (K), square and round shovels (M), garden rake (N), posthole digger (O), hoe (P), carpenter's level (Q), framing square (R), putty knife (S), wood chisel (T), awl (U), socket wrench set (V), hammer (W), rubber mallet (X), pruning shears (Y), metal shears (Z), bar clamps (AA), and pipe clamps (BB).

# PLANTING & WATER MANAGEMENT PROJECTS

# Landscape Beds & Edging

## Tools & Materials

Landscape fabric (optional)
Soil amendments
Mulch
Plants
Hose
Spade
Shovel

**Freeform planting beds** within a landscaped yard provide borders, definition, and visual relief.

**LANDSCAPE BEDS DRESS UP** a plain, green yard and provide supple ground for growing perennials, annuals, vegetables, or whatever greenscape you choose to plant. Use your imagination! Beds can be dug to create borders in an outdoor living room, or they may be positioned as "islands" in a sea of green back yard. The shape, size, and location of a landscape bed is really up to you. Then just add edging to add a polished look to any landscape bed, walkway, or patio area. You can trim a bed with brick, natural stone, timber, or neat-and-clean black plastic edging. Edging serves the practical purpose of containment, keeping surface material in place so it doesn't drift off into the yard. Aesthetically speaking, it creates a visual border and provides an opportunity to incorporate hardscape into a landscape design.

### Create Landscape Beds

Planting areas should occupy 40 to 50 percent of your total open yard area, so don't skimp. Of course, you'll add time to your gardening duties, but more beds means less mowing.

Before digging, use your site map to decide where you will place landscape beds. Don't get boxed into linear designs. Experiment with kidney-shaped beds, or beds that seem to flow like a creek with curved edges. Build in border beds that separate outdoor living spaces, such as a patio, from the rest of the yard. Beds also provide privacy when placed

along a property line and planted with screening varieties, such as evergreens.

Once you decide on bed location and shape, check the soil quality of the area by conducting a soil test. That way you can add the correct soil amendments to be sure you're giving plants the best foundation for growth. Most soil will require amending, and you can do so with organic substances, including: sphagnum peat, wood chips, grass clippings (if you do not use lawn chemicals), straw, or compost. Remember, amendments are mixed into the soil and mulch is placed on the soil, after planting.

In the project shown here, you'll create a landscape bed with curved edges by using a garden hose to outline the bed shape. This bed features plastic edging, which is installed before amending soil. You can choose any number of edging materials (see pages 32 to 37) for this project. As always, before you dig, call your local utilities hotline first.

### Tip

Choose low-maintenance shrubs and perennials that blossom like clockwork each season. Your nursery can help you with good choices for your area. Go on a weekday afternoon when they aren't swamped with weekend shoppers.

1   Use a garden hose to outline the planned garden bed area. Remove the ground cover inside the area with a spade.

2   Dig a trench around the perimeter of the bed using a spade. Place plastic lawn edging into the trench and secure it by driving edging stakes into the bottom lip.

3   Till amendments into the soil with a spade and shovel. Test the design and layout of the plants. Install landscape fabric over the entire area, if desired, to inhibit weed growth.

4   Install plant material. Apply a 2 to 3" layer of mulch over the entire surface. Leave 1 to 2" of clearance for tree trunks and woody ornamentals to prevent insects and pests from attacking them.

# Rigid Paver Edging

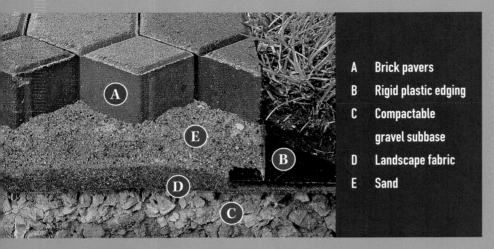

| | |
|---|---|
| A | Brick pavers |
| B | Rigid plastic edging |
| C | Compactable gravel subbase |
| D | Landscape fabric |
| E | Sand |

**Tools & Materials**

Landscape fabric (optional)
Soil amendments
Mulch
Plants
Hose
Spade
Shovel

**Rigid plastic edging** installs easily and works well for both curved and straight walkways made from paving stones or brick pavers set in sand.

**CHOOSE HEAVY-DUTY EDGING** that's strong enough to contain your surface materials. If your patio or walkway has curves, buy plenty of notched, or flexible, edging for the curves. Also, buy 12-inch-long galvanized spikes: one for every 12 inches of edging plus extra for curves.

Invisible edging is so named for its low-profile edge that stops about halfway up the side edges of pavers. The exposed portion of the edging is easily concealed under soil and sod or groundcover.

## INSTALLING RIGID PAVER EDGING

1   Set the edging on top of a compacted gravel base covered with landscape fabric. Using your layout strings as guides, secure the edging with spikes driven every 12" (or as recommended by the manufacturer). Along curves, spike the edging at every tab, or as recommended.

2   Cover the outside of the edging with soil and/or sod after the paving is complete. Tip: On two or more sides of the patio or path, you can spike the edging minimally, in case you have to make adjustments during the paving. Anchor the edging completely after the paving is done.

# Freeform Paver Edging

Brick set on long edges

Brick soldier edging

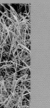

Brick set on faces perpendicular to
the walkway edge

Brick set on faces parallel to the
walkway edge

## Tools & Materials

Flat shovel
Rubber mallet
2 × 4 (about 12" long)
Bricks
Hand tamper
Garden spade
Work gloves
Gravel
Landscape fabric
Eye protection

**BRICK EDGING CAN BE LAID** in several different configurations (see below): on-end with its edge perpendicular to the paved surface; on its long edges; or laid flat, either parallel or perpendicular to the walkway edge.

## INSTALLING BRICK PAVER EDGING

1    Excavate the edge of the patio or walkway site using a flat shovel to create a clean, vertical edge. The edge of the soil (and sod) will support the outsides of the bricks. For edging with bricks set on-end, dig a narrow trench along the perimeter of the site, setting the depth so the tops of the edging bricks will be flush with the paving surface (or just above the surface for loose materials).

2    Set the edging bricks into the trench after installing the gravel subbase and landscape fabric. If applicable, use your layout strings to keep the bricks in line and to check for the proper height. Backfill behind the bricks with soil and tamp well as you secure the bricks in place. Install the patio surface material. Tap the tops of the bricks with a rubber mallet and a short 2 × 4 to level them with one another.

# Concrete Curb Edging

**Tools & Materials**

Rope or garden hose
Excavation tools
Mason's string
Hand tamp
Maul
Circular saw
Drill
Concrete mixing tools
Margin trowel
Wood concrete float
Concrete edger
1 × 1 wood stakes
¼" hardboard
1" wood screws
Fiber-reinforced concrete
Acrylic concrete sealer
Eye and ear protection

**Concrete edging draws a sleek,** smooth line between surfaces in your yard and is especially effective for curving paths and walkways.

**POURED CONCRETE EDGING IS PERFECT** for curves and custom shapes, especially when you want a continuous border at a consistent height. Keeping the edging low to the ground (about one inch above grade) makes it work well as a mowing strip, in addition to a patio or walkway border. Use fiber-reinforced concrete mix, and cut control joints into the edging to help control cracking.

# INSTALLING CONCRETE CURB EDGING

1   Lay out the contours of the edging using a rope or garden hose. For straight runs, use stakes and mason's string to mark the layout. Make the curb at least 5" wide.

2   Dig a trench between the layout lines 8" wide (or 3" wider than the finished curb width) at a depth that allows for a 4"-thick (minimum) curb at the desired height above grade. Compact the soil to form a flat, solid base.

3   Stake along the edges of the trench, using 1 × 1 × 12" wood stakes. Drive a stake every 18" along each side edge.

4   Build the form sides by fastening 4"-wide strips of ¼" hardboard to the insides of the stakes using 1" wood screws. Drill pilot holes to prevent the stakes from splitting. Bend the strips to follow the desired contours.

5   Add spacers inside the form to maintain a consistent width. Cut the spacers from 1 × 1 to fit snugly inside the form. Set the spacers along the bottom edges of the form at 3-ft. intervals.

6   Fill the form with concrete mixed to a firm, workable consistency. Use a margin trowel to spread and consolidate the concrete.

7   Tool the concrete: once the bleed water disappears smooth the surface with a wood float. Using a margin trowel, cut 1"-deep control joints across the width of the curb at 3-ft. intervals. Tool the side edges of the curb with an edger. Allow to cure. Seal the concrete, as directed, with an acrylic concrete sealer, and let it cure for 3 to 5 days before removing the form.

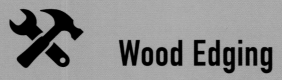

# Wood Edging

**Tools & Materials**
Excavation tools
Circular saw
Compactable gravel
Drill
2× lumber for edging
2 × 4 lumber for stakes
Wood preservative
Landscape fabric
Sand
2½" galvanized deck screws
Eye and ear protection

**Lumber or timber edging** can be used with any patio surface material. Here, this lumber edging is not only decorative, it also holds all of the loose material in place.

**PRESSURE-TREATED LANDSCAPE OR CEDAR TIMBERS** make attractive, durable edging form beds or walkways that are easy to install. Square-edged timbers are best for geometric pavers like brick and cut stone, while loose materials and natural flagstone look best with rounded or squared timbers. Choose the size of timber depending on how bold you want the border to look.

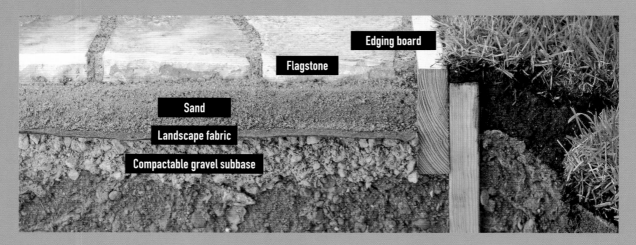

**Wood edging** is a popular choice for simple flagstone or paver walkways and for patios with a casual look.

**DIMENSION LUMBER MAKES FOR AN INEXPENSIVE EDGING MATERIAL** and a less-massive alternative to landscape timbers; 2 × 4 or 2 × 6 lumber works well for most patios and walkways. Use only pressure-treated lumber rated for ground contact or all-heart redwood or cedar boards to prevent rot. For the stakes, use pressure-treated lumber, since they will be buried anyway and appearance is not a concern.

## INSTALLING TIMBER EDGING

1   During the site excavation, dig a perimeter trench for the timbers so they will install flush with the top of the patio or walkway surface (or just above the surface for loose material). Add the compacted gravel base, as required, including a 2 to 4" layer in the perimeter trench. Cut timbers to the desired length using a reciprocating saw with a long wood-cutting blade, a circular saw, or a handsaw.

2   Drill ½" holes through each timber, close to the ends and every 24" in between. Cut a length of ½"-diameter (#4) rebar at 24" for each hole using a reciprocating saw and metal-cutting blade. Set the timbers in the trench and make sure they lie flat. Use your layout strings as guides for leveling and setting the height of the timbers. Anchor the timbers with the rebar, driving the bar flush with the wood surface.

## INSTALLING LUMBER EDGING

1   Excavate the project site, and dig a perimeter trench for the boards so they will install flush with the top of the surface (or just above the surface for loose material). Add the gravel base, as required, including a 2 to 4" layer of gravel in the trench. Cut the edging boards to length, and seal the ends with wood preservative. Cut 2 × 4 stakes about 16" long. Set the edging boards in the trench and drive a stake close to the ends of each board and every 24" in between.

2   Fasten the boards to the stakes with pairs of 2½" deck screws. Where boards meet at corners and butt joints, fasten them together with screws. Use your layout strings as guides for leveling and setting the height of the edging. Backfill behind the edging to support the boards and hide the stakes.

# Planting Trees & Shrubs

**Tools & Materials**

Shovel
Garden hose
Utility knife
Long stake
Tree
Peat moss

**Trees and shrubs are packaged three different ways for sale:** with a bare root, container-grown, and balled-and-burlapped. Bare root specimens (left) are the most wallet-friendly, but you must plant them during the dormant season, before growing begins. Container-grown plants (center) are smaller and take years to achieve maturity, but you can plant them any time—preferably during spring or fall. Balled-and-burlapped specimens (right) are mature and immediately fill out a landscape. They are also the most expensive.

**Tip**
Don't destroy your investment before it is in the ground—protect the branches, foliage, and roots from wind and sun damage during transport.

**TREES AND SHRUBS** are structural elements that provide many benefits to any property. Aside from adding structural interest to a landscape, they work hard to provide shade, block wind, and form walls and ceilings of outdoor living areas. Whether your landscape is a blank canvas or you plan to add trees and shrubs to enhance what's already there, you'll want to take great care when selecting what type of tree you plant, and how you plant it.

A substantially sized tree might be your greatest investment in plant stock, which is more reason to be sure you give that tree a healthy start by planting it correctly. Timing and transportation are the first issues you'll consider. The best time to plant is in spring or fall, when the soil is usually at maximum moistness and the temperature is moderate enough to allow roots to establish. When loading and unloading, lift by the container or root ball, not the trunk. You may decide to pay a nursery to deliver specimens if they are too large for you to manage, or if you are concerned about damaging them en route to your property.

## PLANTING A BALLED-AND-BURLAPPED TREE

1   Use a garden hose to mark the outline for a hole that is at least two or three times the diameter of the root ball. If you are planting trees with shallow, spreading roots (such as most evergreens) rather than a deep taproot, make the hole wider. Dig no deeper than the height of the rootball.

2   Amend some of the removed soil with hydrated peat moss and return the mixture to build up the sides of the hole, creating a medium that is easy for surface roots to establish in. If necessary (meaning, you dug too deep) add and compact soil at the bottom of the hole so the top of the rootball will be slightly above grade when placed.

3   Place the tree in the hole so the top of root ball is slightly above grade and the branches are oriented in a pleasing manner. Cut back the twine and burlap from around the trunk and let it fall back into the hole. Burlap may be left in the hole—it will degrade quickly. Non-degradable rootball wrappings should be removed.

4   Backfill amended soil around the rootball until the soil mixture crowns the hole slightly. Compress the soil lightly with your hands. Create a shallow well around the edge of the fresh soil to help prevent water from running off. Water deeply initially and continue watering very frequently for several weeks. Staking the tree is wise, but make sure the stake is not damaging the roots.

# Windbreaks

**A stand of fast-growing trees,** like these aspens, will create an effective windbreak for your property just a few years after saplings are planted.

WIND SAPS heat from homes, forces snow into burdensome drifts, and can damage more tender plants in a landscape. To protect your outdoor living space, build an aesthetically pleasing wall—a "green" wall of tress and shrubs—that will cut the wind and keep those energy bills down. Windbreaks are commonly used in rural areas where sweeping acres of land are a runway for wind gusts. But even those on small, suburban lots will benefit from strategically placing plants to block the wind.

Essentially, windbreaks are plantings or screens that slow, direct, and block wind from protected areas. Natural windbreaks are comprised of shrubs, conifers, and deciduous trees. The keys to a successful windbreak are: height, width, density, and orientation. Height and width come with age. Density depends on the number of rows, type of foliage, and gaps. Ideally, a windbreak should be 60 to 80 percent dense. (No windbreak is 100 percent dense.) Orientation involves placing rows of plants at right angles to the wind. A rule of thumb is to plant a windbreak that is ten times longer than its greatest height. And keep in mind that wind changes direction, so you may need a multiple-leg windbreak.

## Windbreak Benefits

Windbreaks deliver multiple benefits to your property.:

**Energy conservation:** reduce energy costs from 20 to 40 percent.

**Snow control:** single rows of shrubs function as snow fences.

**Privacy:** block a roadside view and protect animals from exposure to passers-by.

**Noise control:** muffle the sound of traffic or neighbors.

**Aesthetic appeal:** improve your landscape and increase the value of your property.

**Erosion control:** prevent dust from blowing; roots work against erosion.

## Tip

If you live in a rural area, contact your local university extension service for windbreak plans for your area. Also, bulk tree seedlings are available from organizations like the Arbor Day Foundation for very low cost. Of course, seedlings will take longer to mature than saplings, but if you are planting hundreds of trees it might be worth the wait.

1   Before you pick up a shovel, draw a plan of your windbreak, taking into consideration the direction of the wind and location of nearby structures. Windbreaks can be straight lines of trees or curved formations. They may be several rows thick, or just a single row. If you only have room for one row, choose lush evergreens for the best density. Make a plan.

2   Once you decide on the best alignment of trees and shrubs, stake out reference lines for the rows. For a three-row windbreak, the inside row should be at least 75 ft. from buildings or structures, with the outside row 100 to 150 ft. away. Within this 25 to 75 ft. area, plant rows 16 to 20 ft. apart for shrubs and conifers and no closer than 14 ft. for deciduous trees. Within rows, space trees so their foliage can mature and eventually improve the density.

3   Dig holes for tree root balls to the recommended depth (see pages 38 to 39). Your plan should arrange short trees or shrubs upwind and taller trees downwind. If your windbreak borders your home, choose attractive plants for the inside row and buffer them with evergreens or dense shrubs in the second row. If you only have room for two rows of plants, be sure to stagger the specimens so there are no gaps.

4   Plant the trees in the formation created in your plan. Follow the tree and shrub planting techniques on page 39.

# Mulch Beds

## Mulches

**Organic:**
Compost
Lawn clippings (free of chemicals)
Leaves
Wood chips or shavings
Bark
Manure

**Synthetic and Stone:**
Recycled rubber mulch
Stone or brick
Landscape fabric

**Mulch comes in many varieties,** but most is made from shredded wood and bark. Because it is an organic material it breaks down and requires regular refreshing.

**MULCH IS THE DRESSING** on a landscape bed, but its benefits run deeper than surface appeal. Mulch protects plant and tree roots, prevents soil erosion, discourages weed growth, and helps the ground retain moisture. You can purchase a variety of mulches for different purposes. Synthetic mulches and stones are long-lasting, colorful, and resist erosion. They'll never break down. Organic mulches, such as compost and wood chips, will decompose over time.

No matter what type of mulch you choose, application technique is critical. If you spread it too thick it may become matted down and can trap too much moisture. Too thin, it can wash away to reveal bare spots. If it is unevenly applied it will appear spotty.

Consider timing before you apply mulch. The best time to mulch is mid- to late-spring, after the ground warms up. If you apply mulch too soon, the ground will take longer to warm up and your plants will suffer for it. You may add more mulch during the summer to retain water, and in the winter to insulate soil. (As weather warms, lift some of the mulch to allow new growth to sprout.) Spring is prime mulching time.

## Tip

If you have a dog, avoid using the cocoa hull mulch. Some dogs will eat it, and it contains the same dangerous-to-dog chemicals as chocolate.

1   Remove weeds from the bed and water plants thoroughly before applying mulch. For ornamental planting beds it often is a good idea to lay strips of landscape fabric over the soil before mulching.

2   Working in sections, scoop a pile of material from the load (wheelbarrow or bag) and place the piles around the landscape bed.

3   Spread mulch material to a uniform 1" thickness to start. Do not allow mulch to touch tree trunks or stems of woody ornamentals. Compost can double as mulch and a soil amendment that provides soil with nutrients. If you don't make your own compost, you can purchase all-natural products such as Sweet Peet.

**Option:**
Help contain the mulch in a confined area by installing flexible landscape edging.

# Rain Garden

## Tools & Materials

Shovels
Rakes
Trowels
Carpenter's level
Small backhoe (optional)
Tape measure
Wood stakes, at least 2 ft. long
String
6 ft. 2 × 4 board (optional)

**Rain gardens** provide a valuable habitat for birds and wildlife, and these purposeful landscape features also enhance the appearance of your yard.

**A RAIN GARDEN COLLECTS AND FILTERS** water run-off, which prevents flooding and protects the environment from pollutants carried by urban stormwater. In fact, when a rain garden is installed and planted properly, it looks like any other landscape bed on a property. (There are no ponds or puddles involved.) The difference is, a rain garden can allow about 30 percent more water to soak into the ground than a conventional lawn.

Though a rain garden may seem like a small environmental contribution toward a mammoth effort to clean up our water supply and preserve aquifers, collectively they can produce significant community benefits. For instance, if homeowners in a subdivision each decide to build a rain garden, the neighborhood could avoid installing an unsightly retention pond to collect stormwater run-off. So you see, the little steps you take at home can make a big difference.

Most of the work of building a rain garden is planning and digging. If you recruit some helpers for the manual labor, you can easily accomplish this project in a weekend. As for the planning, give yourself good time to establish a well-thought-out design that considers the variables mentioned here. And as always, before breaking ground, you should contact your local utility company or digging hotline to be sure your site is safe.

## Preparing the Land

Soil is a key factor in the success of your rain garden because it acts as a sponge to soak up water that would otherwise run off and contribute to flooding, or cause puddling in a landscape. Soil is either sandy, silty, or clay-based, so check your yard to determine what category describes your property. Sandy soil is ideal for drainage, while clay soils are sticky and clumpy. Water doesn't easily penetrate thick, compacted clay soils, so these soils need to be amended to aerate the soil body and give it a porous texture that's more welcoming to water run-off. Silty soils are smooth but not sticky and absorb water relatively well, though they also require amending. Really, no soil is perfect, so you can plan on boosting its rain garden potential with soil amendments. The ideal soil amendment is comprised of: washed sharp sand (50%); double-shredded hardwood mulch (15%); topsoil (30%); and peat moss (5%). Compost can be substituted for peat moss.

While planning your rain garden, give careful consideration to its position, depth, and shape. Build it at least 10 feet from the house, and not

### Tip: Before you Dig

**Determine the best place for your rain garden by answering the following questions:**

- Where does water stand after a heavy rain?
- What is the water source? (drainpipe, run-off from a patio or other flat surface, etc.)
- What direction does water move on your property?
- Where could water potentially enter and exit a rain garden?
- Where could a rain garden be placed to catch water from its source before it flows to the lowest point on the property?
- Do you need more than one rain garden?

directly over a septic system. Avoid wet patches where infiltration is low. Shoot for areas with full or partial sun that will help dry up the land, and stay away from large trees. The flatter the ground, the better. Ideally, the slope should be less than a 12% grade.

Residential rain gardens can range from 100 to 300 square feet in size, and they can be much smaller, though you will have less of an opportunity to embellish the garden with a variety of plants. Rain gardens function well when shaped like a crescent, kidney, or teardrop. The slope of the area where you're installing the rain garden will determine how deep you need to dig. Ideally, dig four to eight inches deep. If the garden is too shallow, you'll need more square footage to capture the water run-off, or risk overflow. If the garden is too deep, water may collect and look like a pond. That's not the goal.

Finally, as you consider the ideal spot for your rain garden—and you may find that you need more than one—think about areas of your yard that you want to enhance with landscaping. Rain gardens are aesthetically pleasing, and you'll want to enjoy all the hard work you put into preparing the land and planting annuals and perennials.

1   Choose a site, size, and shape for the rain garden, following the design standards outlined on the previous two pages. Use rope or a hose to outline the rain garden excavation area. Avoid trees and be sure to stay at least 10 ft. away from permanent structures. Try to choose one of the recommended shapes: crescent, kidney, or tear drop.

2   Dig around the perimeter of the rain garden and then excavate the central area to a depth of 4 to 8". Heap excavated soil around the garden edges to create a berm on the three sides that are not at the entry point. This allows the rain garden to hold water in during a storm.

3   Dig and fill sections of the rain garden that are lower, working to create a level foundation. Tamp the top of the berm so it will stand up to water flow. The berm eventually can be planted with grasses or covered with mulch.

4   Level the center of the rain garden and check with a long board with a carpenter's level on top. Fill in low areas with soil and dig out high areas. Move the board to different places to check the entire garden for level. Note: If the terrain demands, a slope of up to 12% is okay. Then, rake the soil smooth.

5   Plant specimens that are native to your region and have a well-established root system. Contact a local university extension or nursery to learn which plants can survive in a saturated environment (inside the rain garden). Group together bunches of 3 to 7 plants of like variety for visual impact. Mix plants of different heights, shapes, and textures to give the garden dimension. Mix sedges, rushes, and native grasses with flowering varieties. The plants and soil cleanse stormwater that runs into the garden, leaving pure water to soak slowly back into the earth.

6   Apply double-shredded mulch over the bed, avoiding crowns of new transplants. Mulching is not necessary after the second growing season. Complement the design with natural stone, a garden bench with a path leading to it, or an ornamental fence or garden wall. Water a newly established rain garden during drought times—as a general rule, plants need 1 in. of water per week. After plants are established, you should not have to water the garden. Maintenance requirements include minor weeding and cutting back dead or unruly plant material annually.

# Xeriscape

**Xeriscaping is associated with sand,** cacti, and arid climates, but the basic idea of planting flora that withstands dry conditions and makes few demands on water resources is a valid goal in any area.

**XERISCAPING, IN A NUTSHELL,** is waterwise gardening. It is a form of landscaping using drought-tolerant plants and grasses. How a property is designed, planted, and maintained can drastically reduce water usage if xeriscape is put into practice. Some think that xeriscaping will become a new standard in gardening as water becomes a more precious commodity and as homeowners' concern for the environment elevates.

Several misconceptions about xeriscaping still exist. Many people associate it with desert cactus and dirt, sparsely placed succulents and rocks. They are convinced that turf is a four-letter word and grass is far too thirsty for xeriscaping. This is not true. You can certainly include grass in a xeriscape plan, but the key is to incorporate turf where it makes the most sense: children's play areas or front yards protected from foot traffic. Also, your choice of plants expands far beyond prickly cactus. The plant list, depending on where you live, is long and varied.

## The Seven Principles of Xeriscape

Keep in mind these foundational principles of xeriscape as you plan a landscape design. First begin by finding out what the annual rainfall is in your area. What time of year does it usually rain? Answering these questions will help guide plant selection. Now look at the mirco-environment: your property. Where are there spots of sun and shade? Are there places where water naturally collects and the ground is boggy? What about dry spots where plant life can't survive? Where are trees, structures (your home), patios, walkways, and play areas placed? Sketch your property and figure these variables into your xeriscape design.

Also, carefully study these seven principles and work them into your plan.

1.  Water conservation: Group plants with similar watering needs together for the most efficient water use. Incorporate larger plantings that provide natural heating and cooling opportunities for adjacent buildings. If erosion is a problem, build terraces to control water runoff. Before making any decision, ask yourself: How will this impact water consumption?

2.  Soil improvement: By increasing organic matter in your soil and keeping it well aerated, you provide a hardy growing environment for plants, reducing the need for excess watering. Aim for soil that drains well and maintains moisture effectively. Find out your soil pH level by sending a sample away to a university extension or purchasing a home kit. This way,

you can properly amend soil that is too acidic or alkaline.

3.  Limited turf areas: Grass isn't a no-no, but planting green acres with no purpose is a waste. The typical American lawn is not water-friendly—just think how many people struggle to keep their lawns green during hot summers. If you choose turf, ask a nursery for water-saving species adapted to your area.

4.  Appropriate plants: Native plants take less work and less water to thrive. In general, drought-resistant plants have leaves that are small, thick, glossy, silver-grey, or fuzzy. These attributes help plants retain water. As a rule, hot, dry areas with south and west exposure like drought-tolerant plants; while north- and east-facing slopes and walls provide moisture for plants that need a drink more regularly. Always consider a plant's water requirements and place those with similar needs together.

5.  Mulch: Soil maintains moisture more effectively when its surface is covered with mulch such as leaves, coarse compost, pine needles, wood chips, bark, or gravel. Mulch will prevent weed growth and reduce watering needs when it is spread three inches thick.

6.  Smart irrigation: If you must irrigate, use soaker hoses or drip irrigation (see page 52). These systems deposit water directly at plants' roots, minimizing run-off and waste. The best time to water is early morning.

7.  Maintenance: Sorry, there's no such thing as a no-maintenance lawn. But you can drastically cut your outdoor labor hours with xeriscape. Just stick to these principles and consider these additional tips: 1) plant windbreaks to keep soil from drying out (see page 40); 2) if possible, install mature plants that require less water than young ones; 3) try "cycle" irrigation where you water to the point of seeing run-off, then pause so the soil can soak up the moisture before beginning to water again.

1   Plan the landscape with minimal turf, grouping together plants with similar water requirements. Refer to the Seven Principles of Xeriscape as you sketch. Always consider your region's climate, and your property's microclimate: rainfall, sunny areas, shady spots, wind exposure, slopes (causing run-off), and high foot-traffic zones.

2   Divide your xeriscape landscape plan into three zones. The oasis is closest to a large structure (your home) and can benefit from rain runoff and shade. The transition area is a buffer between the oasis and arid zones. Arid zones are farthest away from structures and get the most sunlight. These conditions will dictate the native plants you choose.

3   Plant in receding layers by installing focal-point plants closest to the home (or any other structure), choosing species that are native to the area. As you get farther away from the home, plant more subtle varieties that are more drought-tolerant.

4   As you plant beds, be sure to group together plants that require more water so you can efficiently water these spaces.

5   Incorporate groundcover on slopes, narrow strips that are difficult to irrigate and mow, and shady areas where turf does not thrive. Install hardscape such as walkways, patios, and stepping-stone paths in high foot-traffic zones.

6   Mulch will help retain moisture, reduce erosion, and serves as a pesticide-free weed control. Use it to protect plant beds and fill in areas where turf will not grow.

7   Plant turf sparingly in areas that are easy to maintain and will not require extra watering. Choose low-water use grasses adapted for your region. These may include Kentucky Bluegrass, Zoysia, St. Augustine, and Buffalo grass.

# Drip Irrigation

## Tools & Materials

Drip irrigation kit
Tubing punch
Extra fittings, as needed

**Drip irrigation systems** offer many different types of fittings, including the spray head shown here. Because they precisely direct water exactly where it's needed, drip systems waste very little water. A thick layer of mulch around plants will help keep soil moist.

**PLANTS LOVE DEEP,** long drinks of water, and this can best be accomplished through water-saving drip irrigation. Rather than dousing plant beds with a hit of water, which can pool on the surface and run off rather than sinking down to feed roots, drip irrigation's misty spray or gurgling drip (depending on the system) take time to feed plants slowly. Not a drop of water is wasted, making this method the most "green" way to water plant beds that require such maintenance.

## Irrigation Equipment

**Some of the things** you'll need include: Emitters (A), Sprayer stakes (B), Crimp (C), Filter housing and filter (D), Key punch (E), Tee fitting (F), Coupler (G), Pressure-reducer (H). **Basic kits come** with only a few components, but can be augmented with pieces purchased "a la carte." You'll also need a punch for piercing the tubing and "goof plugs" for repairing errant punches.

**Tubing for drip irrigation** is thin-wall flexible polyethylene or polyvinyl, typically ¼" or ½" in diameter. Internal diameters can vary from manufacturer to manufacturer, so it's a good idea to purchase pipe and fittings from a single source.

# INSTALLING A DRIP IRRIGATION SYSTEM

1   Connect the system's supply tube to a water source, such as a hose spigot or a rainwater system. If you tap into your household water supply, use a pressure gauge to check water pressure. If pressure exceeds 50 pounds per square inch (psi), install a pressure-reducing fitting before attaching the feeder tube. A filter should also be attached to the faucet before the feeder tube.

2   At garden bed locations, begin installing drip emitters every 18". You can also purchase ½" PE tubing with emitters preinstalled. If you use this tubing, cut the feeder tube once it reaches the first bed, and attach the emitter tubing with a barbed coupling. Route the tubing among the plants so that emitters are over the roots.

3   For trees and shrubs, make a branch loop around the tree. Pierce the feed tube near the tree and insert a T-fitting. Loop the branch around the tree and connect it to both outlets on the T-fitting. Use ¼" tubing for small trees, ½" for larger specimens. Insert emitters in the loop every 18".

4   Use micro sprayers for hard-to-reach plants. Sprayers can be connected directly to the main feeder line or positioned on short branch lines. Sprayers come in a variety of spray patterns and flow rates; choose one most appropriate for the plants to be watered.

5   Potted plants and raised beds can also be watered with sprayers. Place stake-mounted sprayers in the pots or beds. Connect a length of ¼" tubing to the feeder line with a coupler, and connect the ¼" line to the sprayer.

6   Once all branch lines and emitters are installed, flush the system by turning on the water and letting it flow for a full minute. Then, close the ends of the feeder line and the branch lines with figure-8 end crimps. Tubing can be left exposed or buried under mulch.

## Tip

For a fast-drip irrigation solution, use a soaker hose with tiny holes. You can snake the hose through a landscape bed or bury it under mulch. Cut the hose to a desired length and use end caps or hose fittings, as needed. These hoses have a 2- to 3-inch watering width.

# In-Ground Sprinkler System

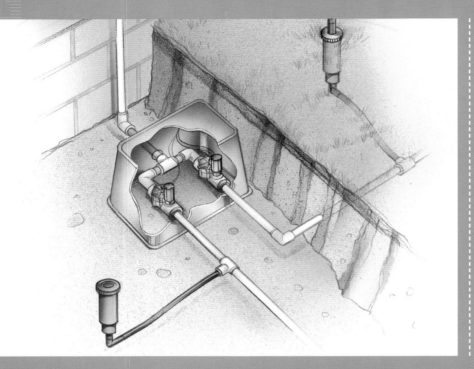

## Tools & Materials

Bucket
Stopwatch
Pressure valve
Drill with 1" bit
Shovel
Utility knife
Compression T-fitting
PVC pipe
PVC valves & fittings
PVC solvent glue
Antisiphon fitting
Irrigation manifold with control
    module & controller
Wooden stakes & string
PVC or PE irrigation pipe
T-fittings & L-fittings
Irrigation risers
Irrigation heads

**Water from the house supply** (or sometimes an external source such as a river and pump) enters a manifold in the irrigation system and is apportioned out to a network of sprinkler heads from the manifold.

**SPRINKLER SYSTEMS** offer a carefree means of keeping your lawn and garden green. Home improvement centers and landscaping retailers sell kits as well as individual components for installing in-ground systems. Installing a system can take a bit of time, but it's not at all difficult. The most challenging part of the job might be tapping into your home's plumbing system. If you're unsure of your abilities here, you can install everything but the final hookups, then hire a plumber to tap into the plumbing system.

For larger yards, design a sprinkler system with several zones, each serviced by a separate feeder pipe. Water is distributed to these zones at a manifold connected to the main supply line.

A variety of timers are available for automating any irrigation system. More expensive models will control as many as 16 different zones, and may have rain sensors that prevent the system from operating if

it is raining. The instructions will vary depending on the type of timer and accessory you buy, but all operate in largely the same way: the timer plugs into an ordinary receptacle, and sends its control signals to the manifold valves through low-voltage wires.

**The manifold** for a sprinkler system typically is buried in a shallow box in the yard and covered with an easily removed lid.

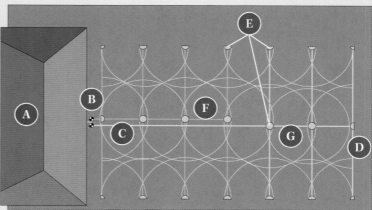

House (A), Valve manifold (B), Sprinkler line (PVC pipe) (C), Sprinkler line (PE pipe) (D), Sprinkler heads (E), Circuit 1 (F), Circuit 2 (G)

1   To measure the flow rate of your water service, set a gallon bucket under an outdoor spigot. Open the faucet all the way and record the amount of time it takes to fill the bucket. To calculate the gallons per minute (GPM), divide 60 by the number of seconds it took to fill the gallon bucket. So, if it took 6 seconds, then 60 ÷ 6 equals 10 GPM. This number will determine the size of your manifold and feeder pipe.

2   Make a sketch showing layout of sprinkler heads. Follow manufacturer's instructions for overlapping head spray patterns. Keep heads at least 6" from sidewalks, driveways, and buildings. Next, mark the irrigation manifold location and create zones for your sprinkler heads. Locate the manifold near the water meter. Zones are individual runs of PVC or PE supply pipe the same size as your water main. Turns and changes of elevation can reduce efficiency, so try to design zones with few turns or rises.

3   Now measure the pressure of your water system. Make sure all faucets in the house are off. Attach a pressure valve to any faucet in the system and open its valve all the way. Record the reading.

## Tip

Before beginning an irrigation system project, check with your local building department. You may need a permit. Also check local requirements regarding backflow prevention or anti-siphon devices. Before you dig trenches, call your utility company to have any utility lines marked.

1   Tap into your water supply. Shut off the water at the main shutoff valve. On the downstream side of your water meter, install a compression T-fitting. To supply the irrigation system, you will need to run PVC pipe to the manifold location. At a convenient location inside the house, install a gate valve with bleed in the line. Outside, dig a 10" trench leading to the manifold location. Drill a 1" hole through the sill directly above the trench, and route the pipe through the hole and down to the trench, using an L-fitting. You may also need to install a backflow prevention or an anti-siphon device between the main and the irrigation manifold; check local code.

2   Choose a manifold with as many outlets as you have zones. The manifold shown here has two zones. Assemble the manifold as directed (some come preassembled, others are solvent-glued) and set it in the hole. Connect the supply pipe from the house to the manifold with an automated control module. Install the controller on the house near the supply pipe (inset) and run the included wires under the supply pipe from the valves to control module.

3   Mark the sprinkler locations. Use stakes or landscape flags to mark the sprinkler locations and then mark the pipe routes with spray paint or string. Once all the locations are marked, dig the trenches. In nonfreezing climates, trenches can be as little as 6". In freezing climates, dig trenches at least 10" deep. Renting a trencher can speed the job considerably. Set the sod aside so you can replace it after the sprinklers are installed.

4   Lay the pipe. Work on one zone at a time, beginning at the manifold. Connect the first section of PVC or PE pipe (PE shown) to the manifold outlet with solvent glue for PVC, or a barbed coupler and pipe clamps for PE (shown). At the first sprinkler location, connect a T-fitting with a female-threaded outlet for the riser. Continue with the next run of PE to the next sprinkler location. Install T-fittings at each sprinkler location. At the end of each zone, install an L-fitting for the last sprinkler.

5   Install the risers for the sprinkler heads. Risers come in a variety of styles. The simplest are short, threaded pipe nipples, but flexible and cut-to-fit risers are also available. Use a riser recommended by the manufacturer for your sprinkler head. For pop-up heads, make sure the nipple is the correct length for proper sprinkler operation.

6   Once all the risers are in place, flush the system. Turn on the water and open the valves for each zone one at a time, allowing the water to run for about a minute or until it runs clear. After the system is flushed, begin installing the sprinkler heads. Thread the heads onto the risers and secure them in place with earth. Make sure the heads are vertical (stake the risers if necessary). Fill in the rest of the trenches and replace the sod.

## Tip

In freezing climates, the system needs to be drained with compressed air before winter. Install the fitting downstream of any anti-siphon valves but before the manifold. In the fall, close the irrigation system's shutoff valve and open any drain valves. At the manifold, open one zone's valve and blow air into the zone until no water comes out. Repeat for each zone.

# BUILDING PROJECTS

**A LANDSCAPE OF PLANTS,** trees, and shrubs is really only a partial landscape. The hardscape—walkways, steps, walls, or fences—guides the eye, demarks boundaries, provides backdrop, and allows for easy access. Small and large yards can benefit from thoughtful inclusion of each of these aspects. A pathway guides visitors to your yard, moving them through the beautiful plantings you have added to your outdoor living area. Fences and walls not only mark boundaries between in and out for privacy and security, they can also provide a contrasting backdrop for plantings or support for vines. Fences also serve as screens to block unsavory elements from view. A retaining wall can help control erosion and provide more level ground for living spaces and planting areas. A decorative low rock wall can

provide seating while setting off patio areas from the yard.

Because the hardscape can tend to be more expensive and labor intensive than some aspects of the vegetative landscape, it is even more important to plan these projects carefully before beginning. Fences and walls on property boundaries are governed by local building codes and respect for neighbors. Make certain to check in with both neighbors and your local governing agency for appropriateness of your project.

To help with planning, begin a list of hardscape elements you observe in your neighborhood and whether you find them appealing or not. Online image searches of walkways, walls, and fences will provide you with more ideas than you may know what to do with.

# Design & Layout for Walkways & Steps

**Tools & Materials**
Stakes
Mason's string
Maul
Plate compactor
Compactable gravel
Excavation tools
Line level
¾" rope
Marking paint
Lumber
    (1 × 2, 1 × 4, 2 × 4)
Level
Drill and drill bit
Cardboard
Screws
Eye and ear protection
Work gloves

**As an important part** of a home's curb appeal, a primary walkway should be styled to complement the house exterior and street-side landscaping.

**Secondary walkways** can be a blend of practicality and decoration. A gentle curve here and there adds interest without slowing travel too much.

**A tertiary path** can be as rustic or creative as you like. It can serve as an invitation to stroll through a garden or an access path for tending plants—or both.

**DESIGNING AND PLANNING** a new walkway starts with a careful assessment of how the path will be used. Landscape designers commonly group outdoor walkways into three main categories, according to use and overall design goals.

The first is a primary walkway: a high-traffic path used by household members and visitors, such as a walkway between the street and the home's main entry door. A main path should provide the quickest and easiest route from point A to point B. Any unnecessary twists and turns are likely to be cross-cut by walkers, leaving you with a less manicured path through the yard. To allow two people to walk side-by-side, a main path should be 42 to 48 inches wide. Surface materials should be durable, slip-resistant, and easy to shovel (if you live in a snowy climate), such as poured concrete, pavers, or flat stones.

A secondary walkway typically connects the house to a patio or outbuilding or a patio to a well-used area in the yard. A comfortable width for single-person travel is 24 to 36 inches. Surfaces should be flat and level underfoot and provide good drainage and slip-resistance in all seasons.

The third type, a tertiary path, is informal, perhaps nothing more than a line of stepping stones meandering through a flower garden or a simple gravel path leading to a secluded seating area. Design tertiary paths for a comfortable stride, with a minimum width of 12 to 16 inches.

Once you've established the design criteria for your walkway or path, spend some time testing the size and configuration of the route to be sure it will meet your needs. See page 82 for a set of stairs for your walkway or landscape.

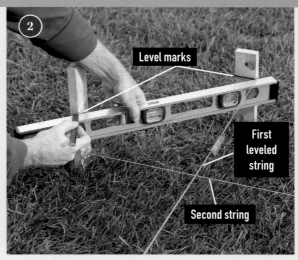

**Level marks**

**First leveled string**

**Second string**

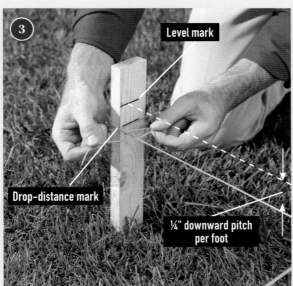

**Level mark**

**Drop-distance mark**

**¼" downward pitch per foot**

1   Use temporary stakes and mason's string to plan the walkway layout. Drive stakes at the ends of each section and at any corners, then tie the strings to the stakes to represent the edges of the finished path. Run a second set of strings 6" outside the first lines.

2   Set up a new string layout to mark the precise borders of the finished walkway. Along the high edge of the walkway, set the strings to the finished surface height. Use a line level to make sure the strings are level. Tip: For 90° turns, use the 3-4-5 technique to set the strings accurately at 90°.

3   Set the border strings lower for the slope. The finished surface follows a downward slope of ¼" per foot on the opposite side of the walkway. Use a homemade slope gauge to set the height of the strings (see step 3, page 62).
   Fine-tune the gravel base to follow the slope setting, and prepare for the sand bed and/or surface material.

4   Excavate the area within the string lines. First, cut sod along the inside edge of the second string line. Remove all grass and plantings from the excavation area. Add the gravel subbase.

1     Experiment with different sizes and shapes for the walkway using two lengths of ¾" braided rope or a garden hose. To maintain a consistent width, cut spacers from 1 × 2 lumber and use them to set the spacing between the rope outlines.

2     Mark the ground with marking paint, following the final outline of the ropes. Excavate the area 6" beyond the marked outline (or as required for your choice of edging). If desired, you can set up a string layout to guide the installation of the gravel subbase (see page 61).

3     Create a slope gauge for checking the slope of your gravel base, edging, or surface material. Tape a level and a drill bit to a straight 2 × 4 that's a little longer than the width of the walkway. The slope should be ¼" per foot: for a 2-ft. level, use a ½"-dia. bit or spacer; for a 4-ft. level, use a 1"-thick spacer. The slope is correct when the level reads level.

## Tip

To plan a simple stepping stone path, cut pieces of cardboard to roughly the same size as an average stone you're using. Lay out the pieces in the desired route, then walk along the "stones" to make sure the spacing is comfortable for walking with a casual stride. Leave the test pieces in place to guide the excavation and/or stone setting.

# PLANNING LANDSCAPE STEPS

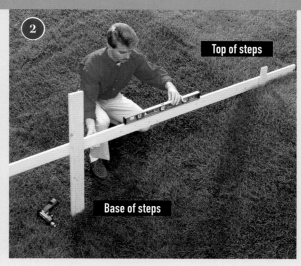

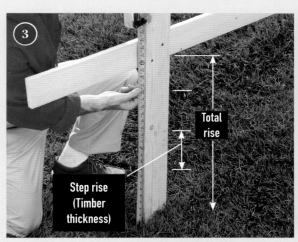

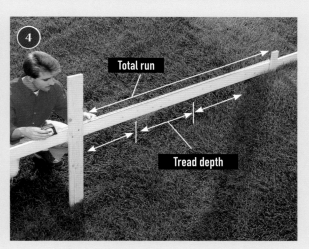

1    Landscape steps are best with a riser height (vertical dimension) of 6" or less and a tread depth (horizontal dimension) of 11" or more. Plan to build each tread with a downward slope of ¼" per foot from back to front. Complete the following steps to calculate the tread and riser dimensions for your steps.

2    Drive a tall stake into the ground at the base of the stairway site. Adjust the stake so it is perfectly plumb. Drive a shorter stake at the top of the site. Position a long, straight 1 × 4 or 2 × 4 against the stakes, with one end touching the ground next to the top stake. Adjust the 1 × 4 so it is level, then attach it to the stakes with screws. For long spans, use a mason's string instead of a board.

3    Measure from the ground to the bottom of the 1 × 4 to find the total rise of the stairway. Divide the total rise by the desired riser height to find the number of steps you need. If the result contains a fraction, drop the fraction and divide the rise by the whole number to find the exact riser dimension.

4    Measure along the 1 × 4 between the stakes to find the total horizontal run of the stairway. Divide the total run by the number of steps to find the depth of each step tread. If the depth is less than 11", revise the step layout to extend the depth of the treads.

# Sandset Brick Walkway

## Tools & Materials

Tape measure
¾" braided rope
Marking paint
Excavation tools
Plate compactor
Mason's string
Stakes
Hand tamp
2- or 4-ft. level
Drill bits
Rubber mallet
Straightedge
Trowel
Masonry saw
Push broom
1 × 2 lumber
Compactable gravel
Straight 2 × 4
Duct tape
Coarse sand
Landscape fabric
Landscape staples
Brick paver units
Plastic patio edging
⅛" hardboard
Paver joint sand
Eye and ear protection
Work gloves
12" galvanized spikes
Maul

**A curving brick walkway** can be as much a design statement as a course for easy travel. Curves require more time than straight designs, due to the extra cutting involved, but the results can be all the more stunning.

**SANDSET BRICK IS A GOOD CHOICE** of material for a walkway for the same reasons that make it a great patio surface—it's easy to work with, it lends itself equally well to traditional paving patterns and creative custom designs, and it can be installed at a leisurely pace because there's no mortar or wet concrete involved. The timeless look of natural clay brick is especially well-suited to walkways, where the rhythmic patterns of geometric lines create a unique sense of movement that draws your eye down the path toward its destination.

In this walkway project, all of the interior (field) bricks are arranged in the installation area and then the curving side edges of the walk are marked onto the set bricks to ensure perfect cutting lines. After the edge bricks are cut and reset, border bricks are installed followed by rigid paver edging to keep everything in place. This is the most efficient method for installing a curving path. Straight walkways can follow the standard process of installing the edging and border bricks (on one or both sides of the path, as applicable) before laying the field brick, as is done in the brick patio project.

With standard brick, you'll need to set the gaps with spacers cut from ⅛" hardboard, as shown in this project.

# INSTALLING A SANDSET BRICK WALKWAY

1   Lay out the walkway curved edges using ¾" braided rope (or use mason's strings for straight sections). Cut 1 × 2 or 2 × 2 spacers to the desired path width and then place them in-between the ropes for consistent spacing. Mark the outlines onto the ground along the inside edges of the ropes with marking paint.

2   Excavate the area 6" outside of the marked lines along both sides of the path. Remove soil to allow for a 4"-thick subbase of gravel, a 1" layer of sand, and the thickness of the brick pavers (minus the height of the finished paving above the ground). The finished paving typically rests about 1" aboveground for ease of lawn maintenance. Thoroughly tamp the area with a plate compactor.

3   Spread out an even layer of compactable gravel—enough for a 4"-thick layer after compaction. Grade the gravel to follow a downward slope of ¼" per foot (most long walkways slope from side to side, while shorter paths or walkway sections can be sloped along their length). Use a homemade slope gauge to screed the gravel smooth and to check the slope as you work (see step 3 in Laying Out Curved Walkways). Tamp the subbase thoroughly with the plate compactor, making sure the surface is flat and smooth and properly sloped.

*continued*

Spacer

Spacer

Spacer

4   Cover the gravel base with professional-grade landscape fabric, overlapping the strips by at least 6". If desired, tack the fabric in place with landscape staples.

5   Spread a 1"-layer of coarse sand over the landscape fabric. Screed the sand with a board so it is smooth, even, and flat.

6   Tamp the screeded sand with a hand tamper or a plate compactor. Check the slope of the surface as you go.

7   Begin the paving at one end of the walkway, following the desired pattern. Use ⅛"-thick hardboard spacers in-between the bricks to set the sand-joint gaps. Tip: It's best to start the paving against a straightedge or square corner. If your walkway does not connect to a patio or stoop, set a temporary 2 × 4 with stakes at the end of the walkway to create a straight starting line.

8   Set the next few courses of brick, running them long over the side edges. With the first few courses in place, tap the bricks with a rubber mallet to bed them into the sand.

## Option:

If your walkway includes long straight sections between curves, set up guidelines with stakes and mason's strings to keep the ends of the courses straight as you pave.

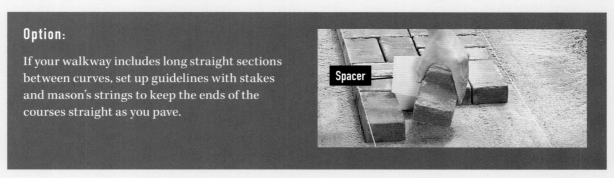

Spacer

*continued*

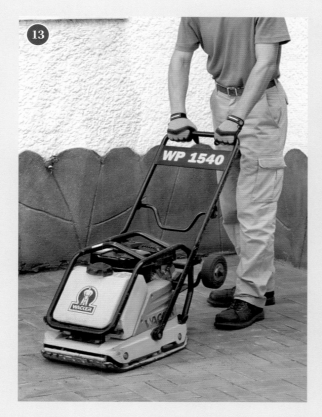

9   Lay out the curved edges of the finished walkway using ¾" braided rope . Adjust the ropes as needed so that the cut bricks will be roughly symmetrical on both edges of the walkway. Also measure between the ropes to make sure the finished width will be accurate according to your layout. Trace along the ropes with a pencil to mark the cutting lines onto the bricks.

10  Cut the bricks with a rented masonry saw (wet saw), following the instructions from the tool supplier. Make straight cuts with a single, full-depth cut. Curved cuts require multiple straight cuts made tangentially to the cutting line. After cutting a brick, reset it before cutting the next brick.

11  Align the border bricks (if applicable) snug against the edges of the field paving. Use a straightedge or level to make sure the border units are flush with the tops of the field bricks. Set the border bricks with a rubber mallet. Dampen the exposed edges of the sand bed, and then use a trowel to slice away the edge so it's flush with the paving.

12  Install rigid paver edging (bendable) or other edge material tight against the outside of the walkway.

13  Fill and tamp the sand joints one or more times until the joints are completely filled. Sweep up any loose sand.

14  Soak the surface with water and let it dry. Cover the edging sides with soil and sod or other material, as desired.

## Variation:

Cut field bricks after installing the edging. Mark each brick for cutting by holding it in position and drawing the cut line across the top face.

# Flagstone Walkway

**Flagstone walkways** combine durability with beauty and work well for casual or formal landscapes.

## Tools & Materials

Excavation tools
Circular saw with masonry blade
Power drill
Masonry chisel
Maul
Rubber mallet
Landscape fabric
Sand
2 × 6 pressure-treated lumber
Deck screws
Compactable gravel
Flagstone pavers
Eye and ear protection
Work gloves

**NATURAL FLAGSTONE** is an ideal material for creating landscape floors. It's attractive and durable and blends well with both formal and informal landscapes. Although flagstone structures are often mortared, they can also be constructed with the sand-set method. Sand-setting flagstones is much faster and easier than setting them with mortar.

There are a variety of flat, thin sedimentary rocks that can be used for this project. Home and garden stores often carry several types of flagstone, but stone supply yards usually have a greater variety. Some varieties of flagstone cost more than others, but there are many affordable options. When you buy the flagstone for your project, select pieces in a variety of sizes from large to small. Arranging the stones for your walkway is similar to putting

together a puzzle, and you'll need to see all the pieces laid out.

The following example demonstrates how to build a straight flagstone walkway with wood edging. If you'd like to build a curved walkway, select another edging material, such as brick or cut stone. Instead of filling gaps between stones with sand, you might want to fill them with topsoil and plant grass or some other ground cover between the stones.

### Tip

Make a flagstone patio to match your flagstone walkway. All the same steps, just make sure the slope is away from house for good drainage.

## BUILDING A FLAGSTONE WALKWAY

1   Lay out, excavate, and prepare the base for the walkway. Form edging by installing 2 × 6 pressure-treated lumber around the perimeter of the pathway. Drive stakes on the outside of the edging, spaced 12" apart. The tops of the stakes should be below ground level. Drive galvanized screws through the edging and into the stakes.

2   Test-fit the stones over the walkway base, finding an attractive arrangement that limits the number of cuts needed. The gaps between the stones should range between ⅜ and 2" wide. Use a pencil to mark the stones for cutting, then remove the stones and place them beside the walkway in the same arrangement. Score along the marked lines with a circular saw and masonry blade set to ⅛" blade depth. Set a piece of wood under the stone, just inside the scored line. Use a masonry chisel and maul to strike along the scored line until the stone breaks.

3   Lay overlapping strips of landscape fabric over the walkway base and spread a 2"-layer of sand over it. Make a screed board from a short 2 × 6, notched to fit inside the edging. Pull the screed from one end of the walkway to the other, adding sand as needed to create a level base.

4   Beginning at one corner of the walkway, lay the flagstones onto the sand base. Repeat the arrangement you created in step 2, with ⅜- to 2"-wide gaps between stones. If necessary, add or remove sand to level the stones, then set them by tapping them with a rubber mallet or a length of 2 × 4.

5   Fill the gaps between the stones with sand. (Use topsoil if you're going to plant grass or ground cover between the stones.) Pack sand into the gaps, then spray the entire walkway with water to help settle the sand. Repeat until the gaps are completely filled and tightly packed with sand.

# Simple Gravel Path

## Tools & Materials

Mason's string
Hose or rope
Marking paint
Excavation tools
Garden rake
Plate compactor
Sod stripper or power sod cutter
Wood stakes
Lumber ($1 \times 2$, $2 \times 4$)
Straight $2 \times 4$
Edging
Spikes
Professional-grade landscape fabric
Compactable gravel
Dressed gravel
Eye and ear protection
Work gloves
Circular saw
Maul

**Loose materials** can be used as filler between solid surface materials, like flagstone, or laid as the primary ground cover, as shown here.

**LOOSE-FILL GRAVEL PATHWAYS** are perfect for stone gardens, casual yards, and other situations where a hard surface is not required. The material is inexpensive, and its fluidity accommodates curves and irregular edging. Since gravel may be made from any rock, gravel paths may be matched to larger stones in the environment, tying them in to your landscaping. The gravel you choose need not be restricted to stone, either. Industrial and agricultural byproducts, such as cinder and ashes, walnut shells, seashells, and ceramic fragments may also be used as path material.

For a more stable path, choose angular or jagged gravel over rounded materials. However, if your preference is to stroll throughout your landscape barefoot, your feet will be better served

with smoother stones, such as pea gravel. With stone, look for a crushed product in the ¼ to ¾" range. Angular or smooth, stones smaller than that can be tracked into the house, while larger materials are uncomfortable and potentially hazardous to

### Tip

Do not use gravel paths near plants and trees that produce messy fruits, seeds, or other debris that will be difficult to remove from the gravel. Organic matter left on gravel paths will eventually rot into compost that will support weed growth. Use a leaf blower to clean light organic material from gravel or wood chip paths.

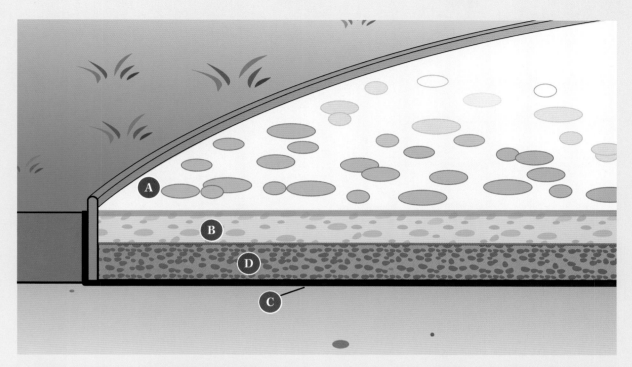

Staked metal edging separates dirt from gravel (A), 2+ inches of gravel forms the walking surface (B), landscape fabric overlaps edging to keep out roots and rhizomes (C), 2+ inches of paver base forms a bed for the walking surface pathway (D).

walk on. If it complements your landscaping, use light-colored gravel, such as buff limestone. Visually, it is much easier to follow a light pathway at night because it reflects more moonlight.

Stable edging helps keep the pathway gravel from migrating into the surrounding mulch and soil. When integrated with landscape fabric, the edge keeps invasive perennials and trees from sending roots and shoots into the path.

A base of compactable gravel under the surface material keeps the pathway firm underfoot. For best results, embed the surface gravel material into the paver base with a plate compactor. This prevents the base from showing through if the gravel at the surface is disturbed. An underlayment of landscape fabric helps stabilize the pathway and blocks weeds, but if you don't mind pulling an occasional dandelion and are building on firm soil, it can be omitted.

### Tip: Make a Spacer Gauge

To ensure that the edges of the pathway are exactly parallel, create a spacer bar and use it as a guide to install the edging. Start with a piece of 2 × 4 that's a bit longer than the path width. Near one end, cut a notch that will fit snugly over the edging. Trim the spacer so the distance from the notch to the other end is the planned width of the pathway.

1   Lay out one edge of the path excavation. Use a section of hose or rope to create curves, and use stakes and string to indicate straight sections (see pages 60 to 63 for detailed steps on designing and laying out a walkway). Cut 1 × 2 spacers to set the path width and establish the second pathway edge; use another hose and/or more stakes and string to lay out the other edge. Mark both edges with marking paint.

2   Remove sod in the walkway area using a sod stripper or a power sod cutter (see option, below). Excavate the soil to a depth of 4 to 6". Measure down from a 2 × 4 placed across the path bed to fine-tune the excavation. Grade the bottom of the excavation flat using a garden rake. Note: If mulch will be used outside the path, make the excavation shallower by the depth of the mulch. Compact the soil with a plate compactor.

3   Lay landscaping fabric from edge to edge, lapping over the undisturbed ground on either side of the path. On straight sections, you may be able to run parallel to the path with a single strip; on curved paths, it's easier to lay the fabric perpendicular to the path. Overlap all seams by 6".

4   Install edging over the fabric. Shim the edging with small stones, if necessary, so the top edge is ½" above grade (if the path passes through grass) or 2" above grade (if it passes through a mulched area). Secure the edging with spikes. To install the second edge, use a 2 × 4 spacer gauge that's been notched to fit over your edging.

5   Stone or vertical-brick edges may be set in deeper trenches at the sides of the path. Place these on top of the fabric also. You do not have to use additional edging with paver edging, but metal (or other) edging will keep the pavers from wandering.

### Option
Use a power sod cutter to strip grass from your pathway site. Available at most rental centers and large home centers, sod cutters excavate to a very even depth. The cut sod can be replanted in other parts of your lawn.

*continued*

6   Trim excess fabric, then backfill behind the edging with dirt and tamp it down carefully with the end of a 2 × 4. This secures the edging and helps it to maintain its shape.

7   Add a 2- to 4"-thick layer of compactable gravel over the entire pathway. Rake the gravel flat. Then, spread a thin layer of your surface material over the base gravel.

8   Tamp the base and surface gravel together using a plate compactor. Be careful not to disturb or damage the edging with  the compactor.

9   Fill in the pathway with the remaining surface gravel. Drag a 2 × 4 across the tops of the edging using a sawing motion to level the gravel flush with the edging.

10   Set the edging brick flush with the gravel using a mallet and 2 × 4.

11   Tamp the surface again using the plate compactor or a hand tamper. Compact the gravel so it is slightly below the top of the edging. This will help keep the gravel from migrating out of the path.

12   Rinse off the pathway with a hose to wash off dirt and dust and bring out the true colors of the materials.

# Pebbled Stepping Stone Path

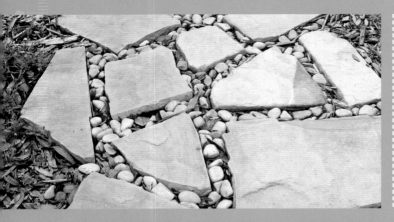

## Tools & Materials

Mason's string
Hose or rope
Marking paint
Sod stripper
Excavation tools
Hand tamp
Wood stakes
1 × 2 lumber
Straight 2 × 4
Edging
Landscape fabric

Coarse sand
Thick steppers or broad
    river rocks with one flat
    face
¼ to ½" pond pebbles
2½"-dia. river rock
Eye and ear
    protection
Work gloves
Level
Rake

**Stepping stones** blend beautifully into many types of landscaping, including rock gardens, ponds, flower or vegetable gardens, or manicured grass lawns.

**A STEPPING STONE PATH** is both a practical and appealing way to traverse a landscape. With large stones as foot landings, you are free to use pretty much any type of fill material in between. You could even place stepping stones on individual footings over ponds and streams, making water the temporary infill that surrounds the stones. The infill does not need to follow a narrow path bed, either. Steppers can be used to cross a broad expanse of gravel, such as a Zen gravel panel or a smaller graveled opening in an alpine rock garden.

Stepping stones in a path serve two purposes: they lead the eye, and they carry the traveler. In both cases, the goal is rarely fast, direct transport, but more of a relaxing stroll that's comfortable, slow-paced, and above all, natural. Arrange the stepping stones in your walking path according to the gaits and strides of the people that are most likely to use the pathway. Keep in mind that our gaits tend to be longer on a utility path than in a rock garden.

Sometimes steppers are placed more for visual effect, with the knowledge that they will break the pacing rule with artful clusters of stones. Clustering is also an effective way to slow or congregate walkers near a fork in the path or at a good vantage point for a striking feature of the garden.

In the project featured here, landscape edging is used to contain the loose infill material (small aggregate), however a stepping stone path can also be effective without edging. For example, setting a series of steppers directly into your lawn and letting the lawn grass grow between them is a great choice as well.

Fieldstone with a flat face

Steppers

## Tip:

Select beefy stones (minimum 2½ to 3½" thick) with at least one flat side. Thinner stepping stones tend to sink into the pebble infill. Stones that are described as stepping stones usually have two flat faces. For the desired visual effect on this project, we chose steppers and 12 to 24" wide fieldstones with one broad, flat face (the rounded face is buried in the ground, naturally).

## MAKING A PEBBLED STEPPING STONE PATH

1   Excavate and prepare a bed for the path as you would for the gravel pathway (see page 72), but use coarse building sand instead of compactable gravel for the base layer. Screed the sand flat so it's 2" below the top of the edging. Do not tamp the sand. Tip: Low-profile plastic landscape edging is a good choice because it does not compete with the pathway.

2   Moisten the sand bed, then position the stepping stones in the sand, spacing them for comfortable walking and the desired appearance. As you work, place a 2 × 4 across three adjacent stones to make sure they are even with one another. Add or remove sand beneath the steppers, as needed, to stabilize and level the stones.

3   Pour in a layer of larger infill stones (2"-dia. river rock is seen here). Smooth the stones with a garden rake. The infill should be below the tops of the stepping stones. Reserve about ⅓ of the larger diameter rocks.

4   Add the smaller infill stones that will migrate down and fill in around the larger infill rocks. To help settle the rocks, you can tamp lightly with a hand tamper, but don't get too aggressive—the larger rocks might fracture easily.

5   Scatter the remaining large infill stones across the infill area so they float on top of the other stones. Eventually, they will sink down lower in the pathway and you will need to lift and replace them selectively to maintain the original appearance.

**Move from a formal space** to a less orderly area of your landscape by creating a pathway that begins with closely spaced steppers on the formal end and gradually transforms into a mostly-gravel path on the casual end, with only occasional clusters of steppers.

**Combine concrete stepping pavers** with crushed rock or other small stones for a path with a cleaner, more contemporary look. Follow the same basic techniques used on page 79, setting the pavers first, then filling in-between with the desired infill material(s).

# Timber Garden Steps

### Tools & Materials
Marking paint
Mason's string
Level
Excavation tools
Hand tamp
Circular saw
Speed square
Framing square
Drill and ⅜" bit with long shaft
Sledgehammer
Wood stakes
Compactable gravel
2 × 4 lumber
Landscape timbers
⅜" landscape spikes
Gravel

**Here we use gravel** (small aggregate river rock), a common surface for paths and rock gardens, for the tread surfaces. Other tread surfaces include bricks, cobbles, and stepping stones. Even large flagstones can be fit to the tread openings.

**TIMBERFRAMED STEPS** provide a delightfully simple and structurally satisfying way to manage slopes. They are usually designed with shallow steps that have long runs and large tread areas, that can be filled with a variety of materials. Two popular methods are shown here—gravel and with poured concrete. Other tread surfaces you might consider are bricks, cobbles, and stepping stones. Even large flagstones can be cut to fit the tread openings.

Timber steps needn't follow the straight and narrow, either. You can vary the lengths of the left and right returns to create swooping helical steps that suggest spiral staircases. Or, increase the length of both returns to create a broad landing on which to set pots or accommodate a natural flattening of the slope. Want to soften the steps? Use soil as a base near the sides of the steps and plant herbs or ground cover. Or for a spring surprise, plant daffodils under a light pea gravel top dressing at the edges of the steps.

Timber steps don't require a frost footing, because the wooden joints flex with the earth rather than crack like solid concrete steps would. However, it's a good idea to include some underground anchoring to keep loose muddy soil from pushing the steps forward. To provide long-term stability, the gravel-filled steps shown here are secured to a timber cleat at the base of the slope, while the concrete-filled steps are anchored at the base with long sections of pipe driven into the ground.

Designing steps is an important part of the process. Determine the total rise and run of the hill and translate this into a step size that conforms to this formula: 2× (rise) + run = 26". Your step rise will equal your timber width, that can range from approximately 3½" (for 4 × 4 timbers or 4 × 6 on the flat) to 7¼" or 7½" (for 8 × 8 timbers). See page 63 for more help with designing and laying out landscape steps. As with any steps, be sure to keep the step size consistent so people don't trip.

## Construction Details: Timber Step Frames

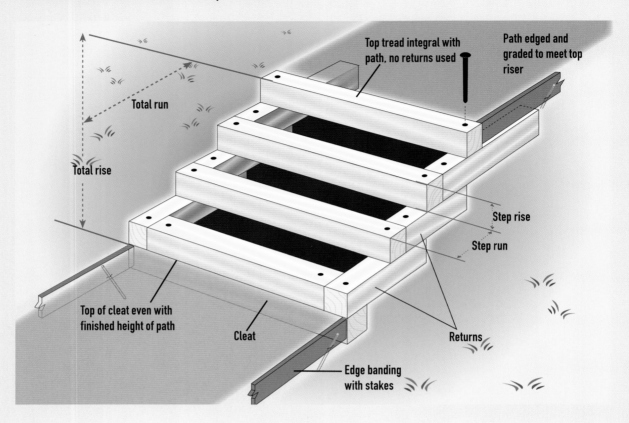

Total run

Top tread integral with path, no returns used

Path edged and graded to meet top riser

Total rise

Step rise

Step run

Top of cleat even with finished height of path

Cleat

Returns

Edge banding with stakes

## Tip: Cutting Timbers

Large landscape timbers (6 × 6" and bigger) can be cut accurately and squarely with a circular saw, even though the saw's cutting capacity isn't big enough to do the job completely. First, draw cutting lines on all four sides of the timber using a speed square as guide. Next, cut along the line on all four sides with the saw set for maximum blade depth. Finally, use a hand saw to finish the cut. For most DIYers, this will yield a straighter cut than saws that can make the cut in one pass, such as a reciprocating saw.

1   Install and level the timber cleat: mark the outline of the steps onto the ground using marking paint. Dig a trench for the cleat at the base of the steps. Add 2 to 4" of compactable gravel in the trench and compact it with a hand tamp. Cut the cleat to length and set it into the trench. Add or remove gravel beneath the cleat so it is level and its top is even with the surrounding ground or path surface.

2   Create trenches filled with tamped gravel for the returns (the timbers running back into the hill, perpendicular to the cleat and risers). The returns should be long enough to anchor the riser and returns of the step above. Dig trenches back into the hill for the returns and compact 2 to 4" of gravel into the trenches so each return will sit level on the cleat and gravel.

3   Cut and position the returns and the first riser. Using a 2 × 4 as a level extender, check to see if the backs of the returns are level with each other and adjust by adding or removing gravel in the trenches. Drill four ⅜"-dia. holes and fasten the first riser and the two returns to the cleat with spikes.

4   Excavate and add tamped gravel for the second set of returns. Cut and position the second riser across the ends of the first returns, leaving the correct unit run between the riser faces. Note that only the first riser doesn't span the full width of the steps. Cut and position the returns, check for level, then pre-drill and spike the second riser and returns to the returns below.

5   Build the remaining steps in the same fashion. As you work, it may be necessary to alter the slope with additional excavating or backfilling (few natural hills follow a uniform slope). Add or remove soil as needed along the sides of the steps so that the returns are exposed roughly equally on both sides. Also, each tread should always be higher than the neighboring ground.

*continued*

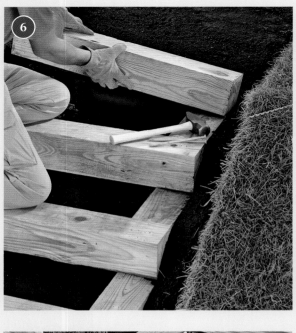

6   Install the final riser. Typically, the last timber does not have returns because its tread surface is integral with the path or surrounding ground. The top of this timber should be slightly higher than the ground. As an alternative, you can use returns to contain pathway material at the top of the steps.

7   Lay and tamp a base of compactable gravel in each step tread area. Use a 2 × 4 as a tamper. For proper compaction, tamp the gravel in 2" or thinner layers before adding more. Leave about 2" of space in each tread for the surface material.

8   Fill up the tread areas with gravel or other appropriate material. Irregular crushed gravel offers maximum surface stability, while smooth stones, like the river rock seen here, blend into the environment more naturally and feel better underfoot than crushed gravel and stone.

9   Create or improve pathways at the top and bottom of the steps. For a nice effect, build a loose-fill walkway using the same type of gravel that you used for the steps. Install a railing, if desired or if required by the local building code.

# Flagstone Garden Steps

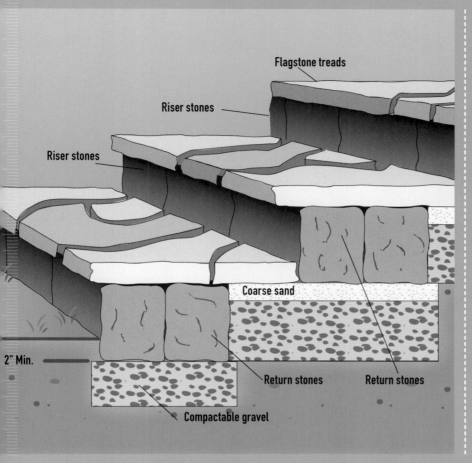

Flagstone treads

Riser stones

Riser stones

Coarse sand

2" Min.

Return stones

Return stones

Compactable gravel

## Tools & Materials

Tape measure
Mason's string
Marking paint
Line level
Torpedo level
4-ft. level
Excavation tools
Maul
Hand tamp
Wood stakes
Lumber (2 × 4, 4× 4)
Straight 2 × 4
Landscape fabric
Compactable gravel
Coarse sand
Wall stone
Flagstone
Stone chisels
Stone and block adhesive
Rubber mallet
Eye and ear protection
Work gloves
Small brush
Banker box
Spade
Granite or polymeric sand

**FLAGSTONE STEPS** are perfect structures for managing natural slopes. Our design consists of broad flagstone treads and blocky ashlar risers, commonly sold as wall stone. The risers are prepared with compactable gravel beds on which the flagstone treads rest. For the project featured here, we purchased both the flagstone and the wall stone in their natural split state (as opposed to sawn). It may seem like overkill, but you should plan on purchasing 40 percent more flagstone, by square foot coverage, than your plans say you need. The process of fitting the stones together involves a lot of cutting and waste.

The average height of your risers is defined by the height of the wall stone available to you. These rough stones are separated and sold in a range of thicknesses (such as 3 to 4 inches), but hand-picking the stones helps bring them into a tighter range. The more uniform the thicknesses of your blocks, the less shimming and adjusting you'll have to do. (Remember, all of the steps must be the same size, to prevent a tripping hazard.) You will also need to stock up on slivers of rocks to use as shims to bring your risers and returns to a consistent height; breaking and cutting your stone generally produces plenty of these.

Flagstone steps work best when you create the broadest possible treads: think of them as a series of terraced patios. The goal, once you have the stock in hand, is to create a tread surface with as few stones as possible. This generally means you'll be doing quite a bit of cutting to get the irregular shapes to fit together. For a more formal look, cut the flagstones along straight lines so they fit together with small, regular gaps.

1   Measure the height and length of the slope to calculate the rise and run dimensions for each step (see page 63 for help with designing and laying out steps). Plot the footprint of your steps on the ground using marking paint. Purchase wall stones for your risers and returns in a height equal to the rise of your steps. Also buy flagstone (with approx. 40% overage) for the step treads.

2   Begin the excavation: for the area under the first riser and return stones, dig a trench to accommodate a 4"-layer of gravel, plus the thickness of an average flagstone tread. For the area under the back edge of the first step's tread and the riser and return stones of the second step, dig to accommodate a 4"-layer of gravel, plus a 1"-layer of sand. Compact the soil with a 2 × 4 or 4 × 4.

3   Add a layer of compactable gravel to within 1" of the planned height and tamp. Add a top layer of compactable gravel and level it side to side and back to front. This top layer should be a flagstone's thickness below grade. This will keep the rise of the first step the same as the following steps. Leave the second layer of gravel uncompacted for easy adjustment of the riser and return stones.

4   Set the riser stones and one or two return stones onto the gravel base. Level the riser stones side to side by adding or removing gravel as needed. Level the risers front to back with a torpedo level. Allow for a slight up-slope for the returns (the steps should slope slightly downward from back to front so the treads will drain). Seat the stones firmly in the gravel with a hand maul, protecting the stone with a wood block.

5   Line the excavated area for the first tread with landscape fabric, draping it to cover the insides of the risers and returns. Add layers of compactable gravel and tamp down to within 1" of the tops of the risers and returns. Fill the remainder of the bed with sand and level it side to side with a 2 × 4. Slope it slightly from back to front. This layer of sand should be a little above the first risers and returns so that the tread stones will compact down to sit on the wall stones.

6   Set the second group of risers and returns: first, measure the step/run distance back from the face of your first risers and set up a level mason's string across the sand bed. Position the second-step risers and returns as you did for the first step, except these don't need to be dug in on the bottom because the bottom tread will reduce the risers' effective height.

*continued*

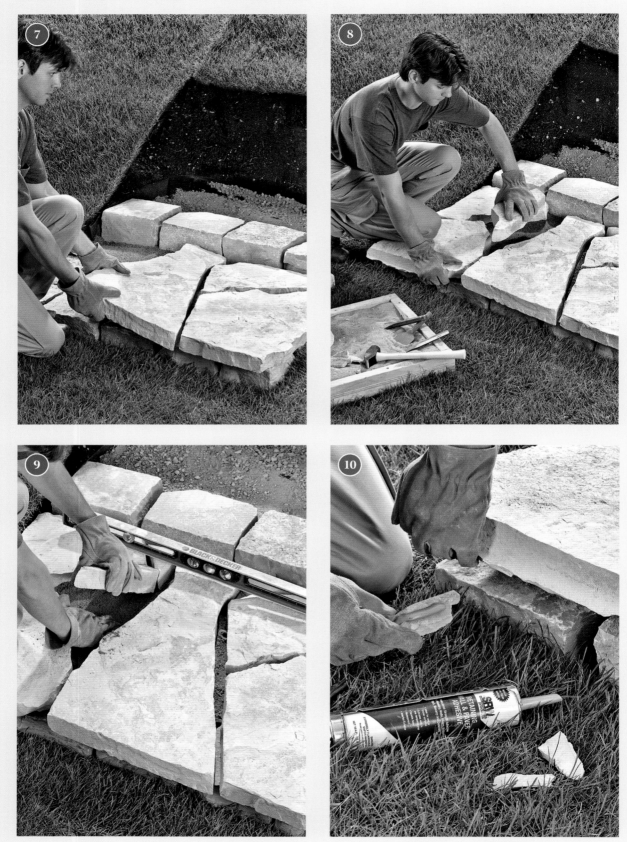

7    Fold the fabric over the tops of the risers and trim off the excess. Set the flagstone treads of the first step like a puzzle, leaving a consistent distance between stones. Use large, heavy stones with relatively straight edges at the front of the step, overhanging the risers by about 2".

8    Fill in with smaller stones near the back. Cut and dress stones where necessary using stone chisels and a maul or mason's hammer. Finding a good arrangement takes some trial and error. Strive for fairly regular gaps, and avoid using small stones as they are easily displaced. Ideally, all stones should be at least as large as a dinner plate.

9    Adjust the stones so the treads form a flat surface. Use a level as a guide, and add wet sand under thinner stones or remove sand from beneath thicker stones until all the flags come close to touching the level and are stable.

10    Shim between treads and risers with thin shards of stone. (Do not use sand to shim here). Glue the shards in place with block and stone adhesive. Check each step to make sure there is no path for sand to wash out from beneath the treads. You can settle smaller stones in sand with a mallet, but cushion your blows with a piece of wood.

11    Complete the second step in the same manner as the first. The bottoms of the risers should be at the same height as the bottoms of the tread on the step below. Continue building steps to the top of the slope. Note: The top step often will not require returns.

12    Fill the joints between stones with sand by sweeping the sand across the treads. Use coarse, dark sand such as granite sand, or choose polymeric sand, which resists washout better than regular builder's sand. Inspect the steps regularly for the first few weeks and make adjustments to the heights of stones as needed.

## FLAGSTONE STEP VARIATIONS

**Pave the slope.** Sometimes the best solution for garden steps is simply to lay some broad, flat rocks down on a pathway more or less as you find it. Make some effort to ensure that the surface of each rock is relatively flat and safe to walk on. Do not use this approach on steep slopes (greater than 2 in 12) or in heavily traveled areas.

**These terraces** are made from large flagstone steppers supported by stacked riser stones. They function as steps in managing the slope, but they look and feel more like a split-level patio. For a natural look and the best visual effect, terrace-type steps should mimic the topography of your yard.

**Cut-limestone** blocks that are roughly uniform in size are laid in a step formation to create a stately passageway up this small hill. A hand-formed mortar cap adorns the sides of the outdoor stairway for a more finished appearance.

**Stacked slabs** cannot be beat for pure simplicity, longevity, and ease of maintenance. The initial cost is high, and stacking stones that weigh several hundred pounds (or more) does require professionals with heavy equipment. But once these lovely garden steps are in place they'll stay put for generations with hardly any attention beyond a simple hosing off.

# Fence Design & Layout

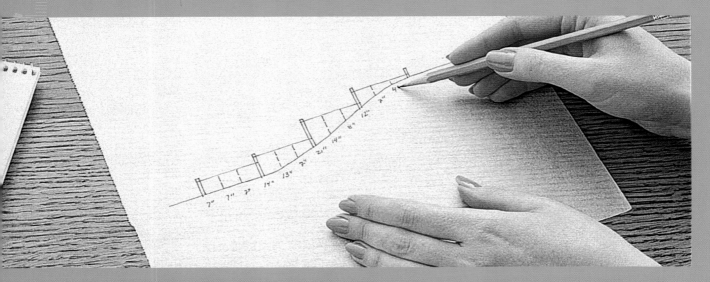

**Use the elevation drawing** described in the Landscape Design & Materials chapter to determine layouts and materials needed for fences and walls that run over uneven terrain.

Good plans make it possible to complete a project efficiently. Plotting fence, wall, and gate locations on paper makes it much easier to determine a realistic budget, make a materials list, and develop a realistic work schedule.

### Tip
Don't start drawing onto your site plan right away. Make a number of photocopies that you can draw on, and save the original as a master copy.

Along with your site map, an elevation chart may be helpful if you have significant slope to contend with. On a copy of the site map, locate and draw the fence or wall layout. Consider how to handle obstacles like large rocks and trees or slopes. Be sure you take into account local setback regulations and other pertinent building codes.

As you begin to plot your new fence or wall, you'll need to do a little math. To determine the proper on-center spacing for fence posts, for example, you divide the length of the fence into equal intervals—six to eight foot spacing is typical. If your calculations

produce a remainder, don't put it into one odd-sized bay. Instead, distribute the remainder equally among all the bays or between the first and last bay (unless you are installing prefab panels).

If you plan to use prefabricated fence panels, post spacing becomes more critical. If you'd like to install all your posts at once (the most efficient strategy), you'll need to add the width of the post to the length of the panel plus an extra half-inch for wiggle room in your plan. But most fence panel manufacturers suggest that you add fence posts as you go so you can locate them exactly where the panels dictate they need to be.

If you're making a plan for building a wall, be sure to plan enough space around the wall itself for footings that are at least twice as wide as the wall they will support. Carefully plot each corner and curve, and allow plenty of space between the footings and obstacles such as trees or low-lying areas where water may collect.

Once you've worked out the details and decided on a final layout, convert the scale dimensions from the site map to actual measurements. From this information, draw up a materials estimate, adding 10 percent to compensate for errors and oversights.

## Handling Slope

It's considerably easier to build a fence or garden wall when the ground is flat and level along the entire length of the proposed site line. But few landscapes are entirely flat. Hills, slight valleys, or consistent downward grades are slope issues to resolve while planning your fence. There are two common ways to handle slope: contouring and stepping.

With a contoured fence, the stringers are parallel to the ground, while the posts and siding are plumb to the earth. The top of the fence maintains a consistent height above grade, following the contours of the land. Most pre-assembled panel fences cannot be contoured, since the vertical siding members are set square to the stringers. Picket fence panels may be "racked" out of square for gentle contouring. Vinyl fence sections generally permit contouring.

Each section of a stepped fence is level across the top, forming the characteristic steps as the ground rises or falls. Stepped fences appear more structured and formal. Pre-assembled panels may be stepped to the degree their bottoms can be trimmed for the slope, or that additional siding (such as kick boards) can be added to conceal gaps at the tall end of the step. Stepped custom-built fences are more work than contoured fences since vertical siding boards must be trimmed to length individually and post heights may vary within a layout.

**Solid planning and careful execution** allow you to turn a sloped yard into a positive design factor when you build your fence or wall project.

## Strategies for Managing Slope

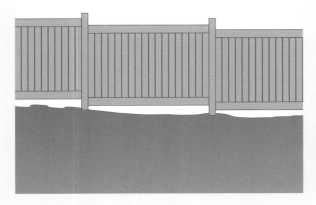

**Stepped panels** are horizontal, maintaining an even height between posts. A good strategy for pre-built panel systems, stepping fences is the only way to handle slope when working with panels that cannot be trimmed, racked, or otherwise altered.

**Racking a panel** involves manipulating a simple fence panel by twisting it out of square so the stringers follow a low slope while the siding remains vertical. Stockade and picket panels are good candidates for this trick, but the degree to which you can rack the panels is limited. If the siding is connected to stringers with more than one fastener at each joint, you'll need to remove some fasteners and replace them after racking the panel.

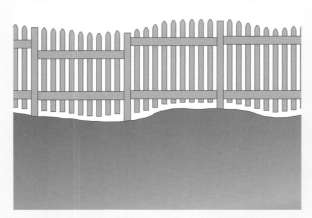

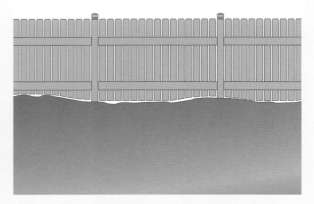

**Contouring creates** a more casual, natural-looking fence. Each individual siding board is set the same distance from the ground below and allowed to extend to full height without trimming. The resulting top of the fence will mimic the ground contour.

**Bottom trimming** creates a level fenceline with a baseline that follows the slope and contour of the land. On low slopes you can use this technique and trim the siding boards on pre-made panels that have open bottoms (in some cases you can raise the bottom stringer). Bottom trimming is best for site-built board and stringer fences, however.

## Contoured Fences

A contoured fence rolls along with the terrain, maintaining a consistent height above the ground as it follows the land. Picket fences and others with individual siding work best for contouring. There are multiple tactics you can use to build a contoured fence. The scenario described below involves setting all your posts, installing stringers, trimming posts to uniform height above the top stringer and then adding the picket siding.

Begin the contoured fence layout by running a string between batter boards or stakes located at the ends and corners of the fenceline, adding intermediate batter boards or stakes as needed to keep the string roughly parallel with the grade. Mark the post centers at regular distances (usually six or eight feet) on the string. Don't forget to allow for the posts when measuring. Drop a plumb bob at each post mark on the string to determine posthole locations. Mark these locations with a piece of plastic pegged to the ground or by another method of your choosing.

Align, space, and set the posts (if appropriate for your fence type). Attach the lower stringers between posts. If you are using metal fence rail brackets, bend the lower tab on each bracket to match the slope of the stringer. Each stringer should follow the slope of the ground below as closely as possible while maintaining a minimum distance between the highest point of the ground and the bottom of the stringer. This distance will vary from fence to fence according to your design, but 12 inches is a good general rule.

Install all of the lower stringers and then install the upper stringers parallel to the lower ones. Make sure to maintain an even spacing between the stringers. Establish the distance from the upper stringer to the post tops and then measure this distance on each post. Draw cutting lines and trim the post tops using a circular saw and a speed square clamped to the post as a guide.

Make a spacer that's about the same width as the siding boards, with a height that matches the planned distance from the ground to the bottom of each siding board. Set the spacer beneath each board as you install it. You'll also want a spacer to set the gap between siding boards. Install the siding and add post caps.

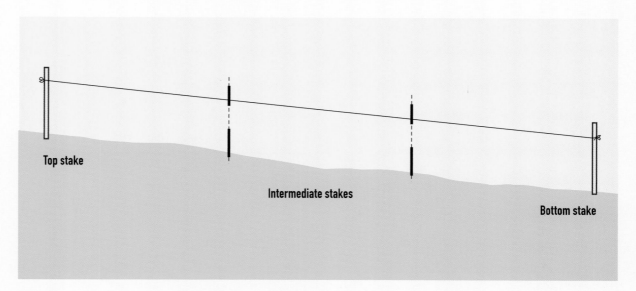

**Slope Option 1: Contour** Contoured fences can follow ground with either a regular slope or an irregular slope. Place a stake at the beginning and end of the fenceline and at each corner. Add intermediate stakes to maintain spacing when the slope changes.

## Stepped Fences

A stepped fence retains its shape and configuration regardless of changes in slope. The effect of the stepping up or down of whole panels is to create a more formal appearance, but it also lets you avoid cutting premade fence panels. The sacrifice is that you often end up with very tall fence posts and you may need to add filler wood between panel bottoms and irregular dips in the ground.

The following stepping technique works over slopes of a consistent grade. If the grade changes much, bracket each new slope with its own stake or pair of batter boards, as in the illustration on the previous page. Treat the last post of the first run as the first post of the second run and so on.

Alternatively, step each section independently, trimming the post tops after the siding is set. The scenario below describes a flat cap stringer, which some fences use to create a smooth top. If this is not needed on your fence, simply measure down the appropriate distances to position the inset or face-mounted stringers.

Begin the stepped fence layout by using mason's string and stakes or batter boards to establish a level line that follows the fenceline. Measure the length of the string from end stake to end stake. This number is the run. Divide the run into equal segments that are between 72 and 96". This will give you the number of sections and posts (number of sections plus one). Measure from the ground to the string at both end stakes. The difference between the two measurements is the rise of the slope. Divide the rise by the number of fence sections on the slope to find the stepping measurement.

Measure and mark the post locations along the level string with permanent marker "Vs" on tape. Drop a plumb bob from each post location mark on the string. Mark the ground with a nail and a piece of bright plastic.

Set the first post at one end and the next one in line. Mark the trim line for cutting to height and run a level string from the cutting line to the next post. Measure up (or down) from the string for the step size distance. Adjust marks if necessary before cutting the posts.

Repeat until you reach the end of the fenceline. Avoid creating sections that will be too tall or too short. The bottom stringer should remain at least four inches above grade.

Cut all posts and then attach stringers or panels so the distance from the tops of the posts to the stringers is consistent.

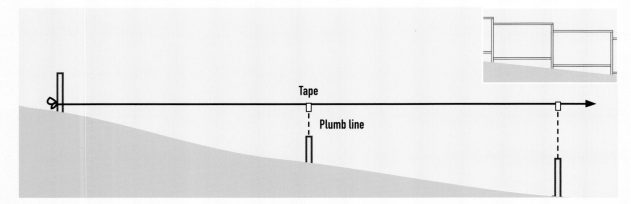

**Slope Option 2: Stepping** Stepped fences (inset) can be installed on either regular or irregular slopes. To plan the fence, run a mason's string between stakes or batter boards at the high end and the low end of the fenceline; measure the distance from the string to the ground at both ends, then calculate the difference between measurements to find the total rise. Divide this amount by the number of fence sections to determine the stepping measurement for each fence panel. On irregular slopes, the amount of drop will vary from section to section.

# Fenceline Layout

**Use a pair** of wood stakes and mason's string to plot the rough location of your fence or wall. Then, for greater accuracy, install batter boards to plot the final location.

### Tools & Materials
Stakes & mason's string
Line level
Tape measure (2)
Level
Circular saw
Hammer
Masking tape
Work gloves
Eye and ear protection
Pencil
Spray paint
Hand maul
1 × 4, 2 × 4 lumber
Permanent marker
Screw gun
Screws

**FENCE INSTALLATIONS BEGIN** with plotting the fenceline and marking post locations. Make a site map and carefully measure each post location. The more exact the posthole positions, the less likely it is that you'll need to cut stringers and siding to special sizes.

For walls, determine the outside edges of the footings along the entire site. Then plot right angles to find the ends and inside edges of the footings.

Laying out a fence or wall with square corners or curves involves a little more work. The key for these techniques is the same as for plotting a straight fenceline: measure and mark accurately. This will ensure proper spacing between the posts and accurate dimensions for footings, which will provide strength and support for each structure.

### Laying out a straight fence
Determine your exact property lines. Plan your fenceline with the locally required setback (usually 6 to 12 inches from the property line). Draw a site map. It should take all aspects of your landscape into consideration, with the location of each post marked.

Referring to the site map, mark the fenceline with stakes at each end or corner-post location.

Drive a pair of wood stakes a couple of feet beyond each corner or end stake. Screw a level crossboard across the stakes six inches up from the ground on the highest end of the fence run. Draw a mason's string from the first batter board down the fenceline. Level the line with a line level and mark the height of the line against one stake of the second batter board pair. Attach a level batter board to these stakes at this height and tie the string to the crossboard so it is taut.

To mark gates, first find the on-center spacing for the gateposts. Combine the width of the gate, the clearance necessary for the hinges and latch hardware, and the actual width of one post. Mark the string with a "V" of masking tape to indicate the center point of each gatepost.

To mark remaining posts, refer to your site map, and then measure and mark the line post locations on the string with marks on masking tape. Remember that the marks indicate the center of the posts, not the edges.

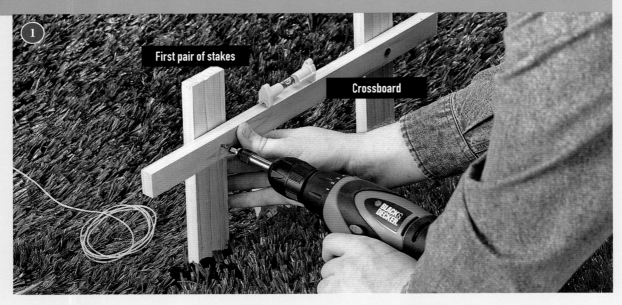

**1**
**First pair of stakes**
**Crossboard**

**2**
**Second pair of stakes**
**Line from first pair of stakes**

**3**
**Post location**

1    To install batter boards, drive a pair of short wood stakes a couple of feet beyond each corner or end of the rough planned fenceline. Screw a level crossboard across one pair of stakes, about 6" up from the ground on the higher end of the fence run. Loosely tie a mason's string to the middle of the crossboard.

2    Stretch the mason's line from the batter board to the second pair of stakes at the opposite end or corner of the run. Draw the string tight, and level it with a line level. Mark the string's position onto one of the stakes. Fasten a crossboard to the second pair of stakes so it is level and its top is aligned with the mark on the stake. Tie the mason's line to the center of the crossboard.

3    Measure out from the starting points of the fenceline and mark post locations directly onto the layout lines using pieces of masking tape (don't forget to allow for the widths of your posts—see opposite page).

## Tip: Spacing for Line Posts and Gate Posts

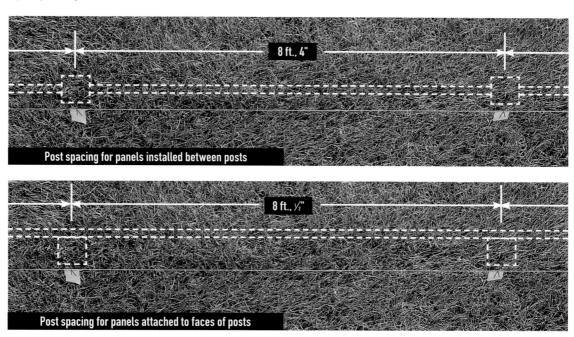

8 ft., 4"

Post spacing for panels installed between posts

8 ft., ½"

Post spacing for panels attached to faces of posts

If your fence panels will be installed between fence posts (top photo) and you are using 4 × 4 wood posts, add 4" to the length of the fence panels and use that distance as the on-center span between posts (the 4 × 4 posts are actually only 3½" wide but the extra ½" created by using the full 4" dimension will create just the right amount of "wiggle room" for the panel). If panels will be attached to the post faces, add ½" to the actual panel width to determine post spacing.

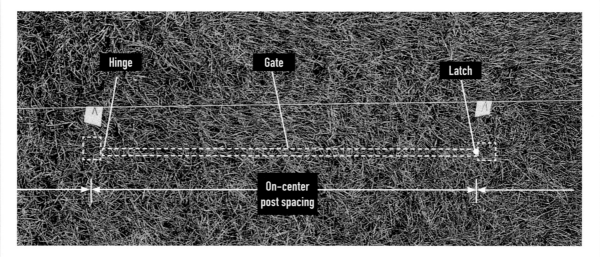

Hinge

Gate

Latch

On-center post spacing

To find the on-center spacing of gate posts, add the gate width, the clearance needed for hinge and gate hardware, and the actual diameter of one post.

## Right Angles

If your fence or wall will enclose a square or rectangular area, or if it joins a building, you probably want the corners to form 90 degree angles. There are many techniques for establishing a right angle when laying out an outdoor project, but the 3-4-5-triangle method is the easiest and most reliable. It is a simple method of squaring your fence layout lines, but if you have the space use a 6-8-10 or 9-12-15 triangle. Whichever dimensions you choose, you'll find it easier to work with two tape measures to create the triangle.

## LAYING OUT A RIGHT ANGLE

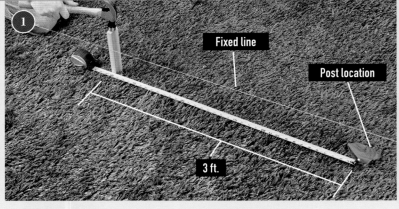

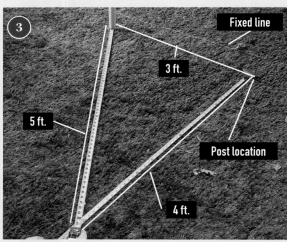

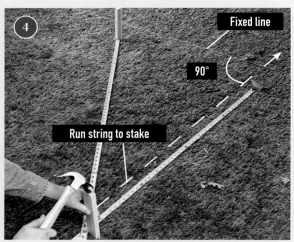

1    Drive a pair of stakes along a known fenceline and run a line that crosses the corner post location (this line should stay fixed as a reference while you square the crossing line to it). Drive a stake 3 ft. out from the corner post location, on the line you don't want to move. You will adjust the other line to establish the right angle.

2    Draw one tape measure from the post location roughly at a right angle to the fixed line. Draw the tape beyond the 4 ft. mark and lock it.

3    Angle the second tape measure from the 3-ft. stake toward the 4 ft. mark on the first tape measure. The two tapes should intersect at 5 ft. and 4 ft.

4    Drive a stake at the point where the tape measure marks intersect. Run a line for this stake to another stake driven past the corner post location to establish perpendicular layout lines. The string tied to the second stake should pass directly over the post location.

## Curves

A curve in a fenceline or wall must be laid out evenly for quality results. One easy way to accomplish this is to make a crude compass by tying one end of a string around a can of marking paint and tying the other end to a wood stake, as shown in step 3 below. The radius of the curve should equal the distance from the compass' pivot stake to the starting points of the curve, so make sure to tie the string to this length.

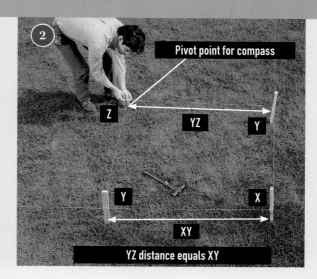

### LAYING OUT A CURVE

**1**

Starting points of curve

90°

Y

Y     X

XY

**XY distance equals radius of curve**

**2**

Pivot point for compass

Z    YZ    Y

Y     X

XY

**YZ distance equals XY**

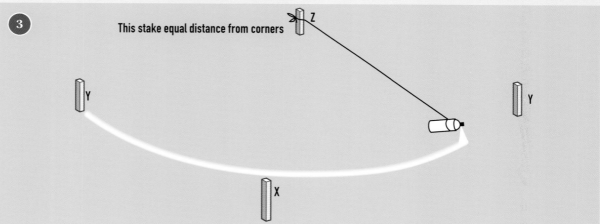

**3**

This stake equal distance from corners

Z

Y

Y

X

1    Plot a right angle at the corner of the outline, using the 3-4-5 method. Measure and drive stakes equidistant from the outside corner to mark the starting points for the curve (labeled "Y" here).

2    Tie a mason's string to each Y stake, and extend the strings back to the corner stake (2). Hold the strings tight at the point where they meet. Then, pull the strings outward at the meeting point until they are taut. Drive a stake at this point to create a perfect square. This stake (labeled "Z" here) will be the pivot point for your string compass.

3    Mark the curve: Tie a mason's string to the pivot point (Z) and to a can of marking paint. When the string is held taut, the can's spray nozzle should be even with the stakes at the start of the curve (Y). Keeping the string taut, spray the ground in a smooth arc, extending the curve between the two Y stakes.

## Setting Posts

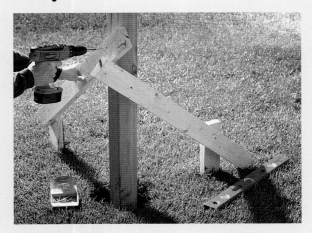

**Taking the time** to make sure posts are vertical and positioned precisely is perhaps the most important aspect of a successful fence building project.

Even among professional landscapers you'll find widely differing practices for setting fence posts. Some take the always-overbuild approach and set every post in concrete that extends a foot past the frostline. Others prefer the impermanence, adjustability, and drainage of setting posts in packed sand or gravel. some treat the post ends before setting the posts, others don't bother. The posts may be set all at once, prior to installing the stringers and siding; or, they may be set one at a time in a build-as-you-go approach. Before deciding which approach is best for your situation, it's a good idea to simply walk around your neighborhood and see how the posts for similar fences are installed, then assess which posts seem to be holding up the best.

Another area of dispute is at which point in the process posts should be cut to length (height). While there are those who advocate cutting all posts before installation and then aligning them in the ground before setting them (especially when installing chain link), the most reliable method is to trim the posts to height with a circular saw or handsaw after they are set in the ground and the concrete has set. Here are some additional thoughts to help you decide how to set your posts:

- Tamped earth and gravel post setting have been increasing the life span and stability of posts for thousands of years by keeping the immediate surroundings of the post drier and firmer.

- The shallow, dish-shaped concrete footing breaks all the rules, but is often the only footing that works in very loose sandy soils. Check with local fence contractors to make sure it's right for your area.

- Hybrid footings help stabilize posts in deep freezing soils. Quick-set concrete mix may be poured into the hole dry, followed by water (or not, according to local custom—soil moisture is sometimes sufficient to harden the concrete).

- Common posts are set high enough to be trimmed down to their final height. Posts with precut mortises (such as split rail fence posts) or finials need to be set to the final height in the hole.

- Dig holes two times the post thickness for sandset or gravel-set and closer to three times the diameter if concrete-set.

- For long-term strength and stability, set all gate posts and end posts in concrete.

The most reliably long-lasting wood posts are pressure-treated with chemicals and labeled for ground contact. species that are naturally rot resistant are unfortunately less so today than in yesteryear.

Once you've plotted your fenceline with batter boards and string, mark and dig the postholes. remove the string for digging, but leave the batter boards in place; you will need these for aligning the posts when you set them.

As a general rule, posts should be buried at a minimum depth equal to 1/3 of the total post length (e.g., a post for a six-foot-tall fence will be approximately nine feet long, with three feet buried in the ground). Check with your city's building department for the post depth and burial method required by the local Building Code. Posts set in concrete should always extend below the frost line.

# Wood Panel Fence

**Building with wood fence panels** is a great time-saver and allows you to create a more elaborate fence than you may be able to build from scratch.

## Tools & Materials

Pressure-treated cedar or redwood
   4 × 4 posts
Prefabricated fence panels
Corrosion-resistant fence brackets
   or panel hangers
Post caps
Corrosion-resistant deck screws
   (1", 3½")
Prefabricated gate & hardware
Wood blocks
Colored plastic
Tape measure
Plumb bob
Masking tape
Stakes and mason's string
Clamshell digger or power auger
Gravel
Hand tamp
Level
2 × 4 lumber
Circular saw, hand saw, or
   reciprocating saw
Concrete
Drill
Line level
Clamps
Scrap lumber
Shovel
Hammer
Speed square
Eye and ear protection
Work gloves
Permanent marker
Hinges (3)

**PREFABRICATED FENCE PANELS** take much of the work out of putting up a fence, and (surprisingly) using them is often less expensive than building a board and stringer fence from scratch. They are best suited for relatively flat yards, but may be stepped down on slopes that aren't too steep.

Fence panels come in many styles, ranging from privacy to picket. Most tend to be built lighter than fences you'd make from scratch, with thinner wood for the stringers and siding. When shopping for panels, compare quality and heft of lumber and fasteners as well as cost.

Purchase panels, gate hardware, and gate (if you're not building one) before setting and trimming your posts. Determine also if panels can be trimmed or reproduced from scratch for short sections.

The most exacting task when building a panel fence involves insetting the panels between the posts. This requires that preset posts be precisely spaced and perfectly plumb. In our inset panel sequence, we set one post at a time as the fence was built, so the attached panel position can determine the spacing, not the preset posts.

An alternative installation to setting panels between posts is to attach them to the post faces. Face-mounted panels are more forgiving of preset posts, since the attachment point of stringers doesn't need to be dead center on the posts.

Wood fence panels usually are constructed in either six- or eight-foot lengths. Cedar and pressure treated pine are the most common wood types used in making fence panels, although you may also find redwood in some areas. Generally, the cedar panels cost one-and-a-half to two times as much for similar styles in pressure-treated lumber.

When selecting wood fence panels, inspect every board in each panel carefully (and be sure to check both sides of the panel). These products are fairly susceptible to damage during shipping.

## PANEL BOARD PATTERN VARIATIONS

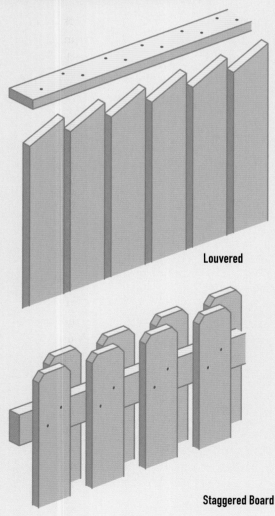

**Louvered**

**Staggered Board**

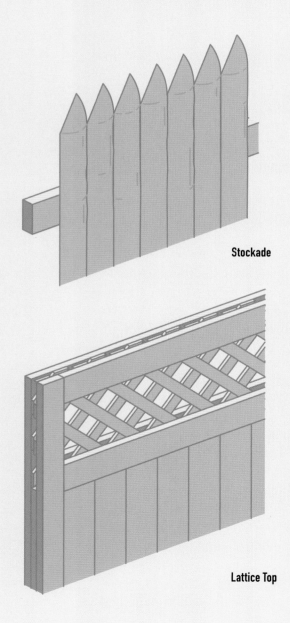

**Stockade**

**Lattice Top**

# Tips for Installing Fence Panels

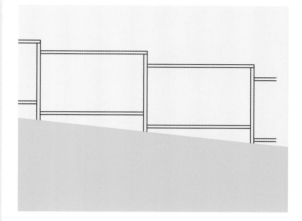

**On a sloped lot,** install the panels in a step pattern, trying to keep a consistent vertical drop between panels. It is difficult to cut most preassembled panels, so try to plan the layout so only full-width panels are used.

**Metal fence panel hangers** make quick work of hanging panels and offer a slight amount of wiggle room if the panel is up to ½" narrower than the space between posts.

Flatten tab when installling hanger

**With some panel styles,** the best tactic is to flatten the lower tab after attaching it to the post and then bend it up or down against the panel frame once the panel is in place.

**Setting all of the posts** in concrete at one time and then installing the panels after the concrete sets has advantages as well as disadvantages. On the plus side, this approach lets you pour all of the concrete at the same time and provides good access so you can make absolutely certain the posts are level and plumb. On the downside, if the post spacing is off even a little bit, you'll need to trim the panel (which can be tricky) or attach a shim to the post or the panel frame (also tricky). Most panel manufacturers recommend installing the posts as you go.

1   Lay out the fenceline, and mark the posthole locations with colored plastic (inset). Space the holes to fit the fence panels, adding the actual post width (3½" for 4 × 4 posts) plus ¼" for brackets to the panel length. Tip: For stepped fences, measure the spacing along a level line, not along the slope.

2   Dig the first posthole for a corner or end post using a clamshell digger or power auger. Add 6" of gravel to the hole, and tamp it flat. Set, plumb, and brace the first post with cross bracing.

3   Dig the second posthole using a 2 × 4 spacer to set the distance between posts (cut the spacer to the same length as the stringers on the preassembled fence panels).

4   Fill the first posthole with concrete or with tamped soil and gravel. Tamp the concrete with a 2 × 4 as you fill the hole. Let the concrete set.

5   Install the stringer brackets onto the first post using corrosion-resistant screws or nails. Shorter fences may have two brackets, while taller fences typically have three. Note: The bottom of the fence siding boards should be at least 2" above the ground when the panel is installed.

6   Set the first panel into the brackets. Shim underneath the free end of the panel with scrap lumber so that the stringers are level and the panel is properly aligned with the fenceline. Fasten the panel to the brackets with screws or nails.

7   Mark the second post for brackets. Set the post in its hole and hold it against the fence panel. Mark the positions of the panel stringers for installing the brackets. Remove the post and install the stringer brackets, as before.

8   Reset the second post, slipping the ends of the panel stringers into the brackets. Brace the post so it is plumb, making sure the panel remains level and is aligned with the fenceline. Fasten the brackets to the panel with screws or nails.

9   Anchor the second post in concrete. After the concrete sets, continue building the fence, following steps 5 to 8. Option: You can wait to fill the remaining postholes with concrete until all of the panels are in place.

10  Attach the post caps after trimming the posts to their finished height (use a level mason's line to mark all of the posts at the same height). Install the gate, if applicable; see next page.

1   To install a prefabricated gate, attach three evenly spaced hinges to the gate frame using corrosion-resistant screws.

2   Follow the hardware manufacturer's directions, making sure the hinge pins are straight and parallel with the edge of the gate. Position the gate between the gate posts so the hinge pins rest against one post. Shim the gate to the desired height using wood blocks set on the ground. Make sure there is an even gap (reveal) between the gate and the latch post, and then fasten the hinges to the hinge post with screws (inset).

# Split Rail Fence

## Tools & Materials

Mason's string
Shovel
Clamshell digger or power auger
Digging bar (with tamping head)
    or 2 × 4
Level
Reciprocating saw or handsaw
Tape measure
Stakes
Soil
Nails
Precut split rail fence posts and rails
Compactable gravel
Plastic tags
Lumber and screws for cross bracing
Wheelbarrow
Line level
Shovel
Eye and ear protection
Work gloves

**A split rail fence** looks great as a garden backdrop or a friendly boundary line. The rough-hewn texture and traditional wood joints are reminiscent of homesteaders' fences built from lumber cut and dressed right on the property.

**THE SPLIT RAIL,** or post and rail, fence is essentially a rustic version of the post and board fence style and is similarly a good choice for a decorative accent, for delineating areas, or for marking boundaries without creating a solid visual barrier. Typically made from split cedar logs, the fence materials have naturally random shaping and dimensions, with imperfect details and character marks that give the wood an appealing hand-hewn look. Natural weathering of the untreated wood only enhances the fence's rustic beauty.

The construction of a split rail fence couldn't be simpler. The posts have holes or notches (called mortises) cut into one or two facets. The fence rails have trimmed ends (called tenons) that fit into the mortises. No fasteners are needed. Posts come in three types to accommodate any basic configuration: common posts have through mortises, end posts have half-depth mortises on one facet, and corner posts

have half-depth mortises on two adjacent facets. The two standard fence styles are two-rail, which stand about three feet tall, and three-rail, which stand about four feet tall. Rails are commonly available in eight- and ten-feet lengths.

In keeping with the rustic simplicity of the fence design, split rail fences are typically installed by setting the posts with tamped soil and gravel instead of concrete footings (frost heave is generally not a concern with this fence, since the joints allow for plenty of movement). This comes with a few advantages: the postholes are relatively small, you save the expense of concrete, and it's much easier to replace a post if necessary. Plan to bury about a third of the total post length (or 24 inches minimum). This means a three-foot-tall fence should have 60-inch long posts. If you can't find long posts at your local home center, try a lumberyard or fencing supplier.

Earth

Gravel

1   Determine the post spacing by dry-assembling a fence section and measuring the distance between the post centers. Be sure the posts are square to the rails before measuring.

2   Set up a string line using mason's string and stakes to establish the fence's path, including any corners and return sections. Mark each post location along the path using a nail and plastic tag.

3   Dig the postholes so they are twice as wide as the posts and at a depth equal to ⅓ the total post length plus 6". Because split posts vary in size, you might want to lay out the posts beforehand and dig each hole according to the post size.

4   Add 6" of drainage gravel to each posthole. Tamp the gravel thoroughly with a digging bar or a 2 × 4 so the layer is flat and level.

5   Set and measure the first post. Drop the post in its hole, and then hold it plumb while you measure from the ground to the desired height. If necessary, add or remove gravel and re-tamp to adjust the post height.

6   Brace the post with cross bracing so it is plumb. Add 2" of gravel around the bottom of the post. Tamp the gravel with a digging bar or 2 × 4, being careful not to disturb the post.

7   Fill and tamp around the post, one layer at a time. Alternate between 4" of soil and 2" of gravel (inset), tamping each layer all the way around the post before adding the next layer. Check the post for plumb as you work. Overfill the top of the hole with soil and tamp it into a hard mound to help shed water.

8   Assemble the first section of fence by setting the next post in its hole and checking its height. Fit the rails into the post mortises, and then brace the second post in place. Note: Set all the posts at the same height above grade for a contoured fence.

9   Secure the second post by filling and tamping with alternate layers of gravel and soil, as with the first post. Repeat steps 5 through 9 to complete the fence. Tip: Set up a mason's string to help keep the posts in a straight line as you set them.

## Variation
For a fence that remains level across the top, set up a level mason's line strung between two installed fence posts or between temporary supports. Set all of the posts so their tops are just touching the line.

## Tip: Custom Details

Custom-cut your rails to build shorter fence sections. Cut the rails to length using a reciprocating saw and long wood blade or a handsaw (be sure to factor in the tenon when determining the overall length). To cut the tenon, make a cardboard template that matches the post mortises. Use the template to mark the tenon shape onto the rail end, and then cut the tenon to fit.

Gates for split rail fences are available from fencing suppliers in standard and custom-order sizes. Standard sizes include 4 ft. for a walk-through entrance gate and 8 or 10 ft. for a drive-through gate. For large gates, set the side posts in concrete footings extending below the frost line.

# Vinyl Panel Fence

## Tools & Materials

Mason's string
Shovel
Clamshell digger or power auger
Circular saw
Drill
Tape measure
Hand maul
Line level
Post level
Clamps or duct tape
Concrete tools
Stakes
2 × 4 lumber
Vinyl fence materials (with
    hardware, fasteners, and
    decorative accessories)
Pea gravel
Concrete
Pressure-treated 4 × 4 (for gate,
    if applicable)
PVC cement or screws (optional)
Work gloves
Post caps
Eye and ear protection

Vinyl fencing is now available in a wide range of traditional designs, including picket, post and board, open rail, and solid panel. Color options are generally limited to various shades of white, tan, and gray.

**THE BEST FEATURES** of vinyl fencing are its resilience and durability. Vinyl fencing is made with a form of tough, weather-resistant, UV-protected PVC (polyvinyl chloride), a plastic compound that's found in numerous household products, from plumbing pipe to shower curtains. A vinyl fence never needs to be painted and should be guaranteed for decades not to rot, warp, or discolor. So if you like the styling of traditional wood fences, but minimal maintenance is a primary consideration, vinyl might just be your best option. Another good option is wood composite fencing, which comes in fewer styles than vinyl but is environmentally friendly and can replicate the look of wood fencing.

Installing most vinyl fencing is similar to building a wood panel fence. With both materials, it's safest to set the posts as you go, using the infill panels to help you position the posts. Accurate post placement is critical with vinyl, because many types of panels cannot be trimmed if the posts are too close together. Squeezing the panel in can lead to buckling when the vinyl expands on hot days, while setting the posts too far apart results in unsightly gaps.

Given the limited workability of most vinyl panels, this fencing tends to work best on level or gently sloping ground. Keep in mind that installation of vinyl fences varies widely by manufacturer and fence style.

Post height string

Fence hinge string

1  Lay out the first run of fence with stakes and mason's string. Position the string so it represents the outside or inside faces of the posts (you'll use layout strings to align the posts throughout the installation). Mark the center of the first post hole by measuring in from the string half the post width.

2  Dig the first posthole, following the manufacturer's requirements for diameter and depth (improper hole dimensions can void the warranty). Add 4 to 6" (or as directed) of pea gravel to the bottom of the hole and tamp it down so it is flat and level using a 2 × 4 or 4 × 4.

3  Attach the fence panel brackets to the first post using the provided screws. Dry-fit a fence panel into the brackets, then measure from the top of the post to the bottom edge of the panel. Add 2" (or as directed) to represent the distance between the fence and the ground; the total dimension is the posts' height above the ground.

4  Set up a post-top string to guide the post installation. Using the post height dimension, tie a mason's string between temporary 2 × 4 supports so the string is centered over the post locations. Use a line level to make sure the string is level. Measure from the string to the ground in several places to make sure the height is suitable along the entire fence run.

5  Set the first post. Drop the post in its hole and align it with the fenceline string and height string. Install cross bracing to hold the post perfectly plumb. Tip: Secure bracing boards to the post with spring-type clamps or duct tape. Fill the posthole with concrete and let it set completely.

6  Determine the second post's location by fitting a fence panel into the brackets on the first post. Mark the ground at the free edge of the panel. Measure out from the mark half the post width to find the center of the post hole (accounting for any additional room needed for the panel brackets).

7  Complete the fence section. Dig the hole for the second post, add gravel, and tamp as before. Attach the panel brackets to the second post, set the post in place, and check its height against the string line. Assemble the fence section with the provided screws (inset). Confirm that the fence panel is level. Brace the second post in place (as shown) and anchor it with concrete. Repeat the same layout and construction steps to build the remaining fence sections.

*continued*

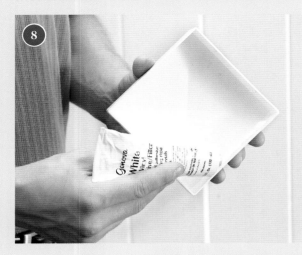

8   Add the post caps. Depending on the product, caps may be installed with PVC cement or screws, or they may be fitted without fasteners. Add any additional decorative accessories, such as screw caps, to complete the installation.

9   Hang the gate using the provided hardware. Fasten the hinges to the gate panel with screws. Position the gate in line with the infill fence panels, and screw the hinges to the hinge post. Install the latch hardware onto the gate and latch post. Close the gate, position the gate stops against the gate rails, and fasten the stops to the latch post with screws.

 Reinforce the hinge post with a pressure-treated 4 × 4 inserted inside the post. Set the post in concrete following the same steps used for fence sections. Check carefully to make sure the post is plumb, as this will ensure the gate swings properly. Install the latch post according to the manufacturer's specified dimension for the gate opening.

### Tip: Cutting Panels
Cut panels for short runs on solid-panel fencing (if straight along the top) per manufacturer's recommendations.

# Dry Stone Wall

## Tools & Materials
Mason's string and stakes
Compactable gravel
Ashlar stone
Capstones
Mortar mix
Trowel
Stiff-bristle brush
Work gloves
Protective footwear

**It is easiest** to build a dry stone wall with ashlar—stone that has been split into roughly rectangular blocks. Ashlar stone is stacked in the same running-bond pattern used in brick wall construction; each stone overlaps a joint in the previous course. This technique avoids long vertical joints, resulting in a wall that is attractive and also strong.

**STONE WALLS** are beautiful, long-lasting structures that are surprisingly easy to build, provided you plan carefully. A low stone wall can be constructed without mortar using a centuries-old method known as dry laying. With this technique, the wall is actually formed by two separate stacks that lean together slightly. The position and weight of the two stacks support each other, forming a single, sturdy wall. A dry stone wall can be built to any length, but its width must be at least half of its height.

You can purchase stone for this project from a quarry or stone supplier, where different sizes, shapes, and colors of stone are sold, priced by the ton. The quarry or stone center can also sell you Type M mortar—necessary for bonding the capstones to the top of the wall.

Building dry stone walls requires patience and a fair amount of physical effort. The stones must be sorted by size and shape. You'll probably also need to shape some of the stones to achieve consistent spacing and a general appearance that appeals to you.

To shape a stone, score it using a circular saw outfitted with a masonry blade. Place a mason's chisel on the score line and strike with a maul until the stone breaks. Wear safety glasses when using stonecutting tools.

Shaping stones
(½ wall width)

Filler Stones

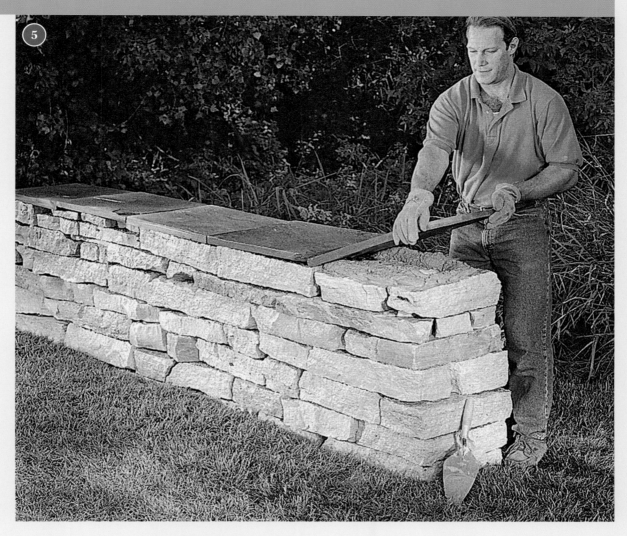

1.    Lay out the wall site using stakes and mason's string. Dig a 6"-deep trench that extends 6" beyond the wall on all sides. Add a 4" crushed stone sub-base to the trench, creating a "V" shape by sloping the sub-base so the center is about 2" deeper than the edges.

2.    Select appropriate stones and lay the first course. Place pairs of stones side by side, flush with the edges of the trench and sloping toward the center. Use stones of similar height; position uneven sides face down. Fill any gaps between the shaping stones with small filler stones.

3.    Lay the next course, staggering the joints. Use pairs of stones of varying lengths to offset the center joint. Alternate stone length, and keep the height even, stacking pairs of thin stones if necessary to maintain consistent height. Place filler stones in the gaps.

4.    Every other course, place a tie stone every 3 ft. You may need to split the tie stones to length. Check the wall periodically for level.

5.    Mortar the capstones to the top of the wall, keeping the mortar at least 6" from the edges so it's not visible. Push the capstones together and mortar the cracks in between. Brush off dried excess mortar with a stiff-bristle brush.

# Interlocking Block Retaining Wall

**Interlocking concrete** block is the only retaining wall material that comes ready to install. With little or no cutting, you can build a wall with straight lines, curves, or steps, or have it conform to a slope on one or both ends.

## Tools & Materials

Wheelbarrow
Shovel
Line level
Hand tamper
Tamping machine (available for rent)
Small maul
Masonry chisel
Eye and ear protection
Work gloves
4-ft. level
Tape measure
Caulk gun
Circular saw with masonry cutting blade
Stakes
Mason's string
Landscape fabric
Compactable gravel
Perforated drain pipe
Coarse backfill material
Construction adhesive
Excavation tools
Interlocking block
Flour or marking paint

**SLOPING AREAS** of a yard may be fun for the kids to play on, but they can certainly limit your usable space for amenities like patios and gardens. When you need more flat ground or simply want to reshape nature's contours a bit, a low retaining wall is the answer. Retaining walls cut into a slope—and in some cases, replace the slope—bridging the upper and lower levels while adding more useable area to both.

Low retaining walls can be built with a variety of materials, including landscape timbers, natural stone, and poured concrete. But by far the most popular material for do-it-yourself projects is interlocking concrete block made specifically for retaining walls. This block requires no mortar—most types are simply stacked in ordered rows—and it has flanges (or pins) that automatically set the batter for the wall (the backward lean that most retaining walls have for added strength). Interlocking block is available at home and garden centers and landscape suppliers. Most types have roughly textured faces to mimic the look of natural stone.

Due to the structural factors involved, the recommended height limit for do-it-yourself retaining walls is three feet. Anything higher is best left to a professional. As walls get taller, the physical stresses involved and resulting potential problems rise dramatically. Retaining walls of any size may be governed by the local Building Code; contact your city's building department to learn about construction specifications and permit requirements.

## Options for Positioning a Retaining Wall

Structural features for all retaining walls include: a compactable gravel subbase to make a solid footing for the wall, crushed stone backfill, a perforated drain pipe to improve drainage behind the wall, and landscape fabric to keep the loose soil from washing into and clogging the gravel backfill. There are a couple different ways you can position a retaining wall on your slope:

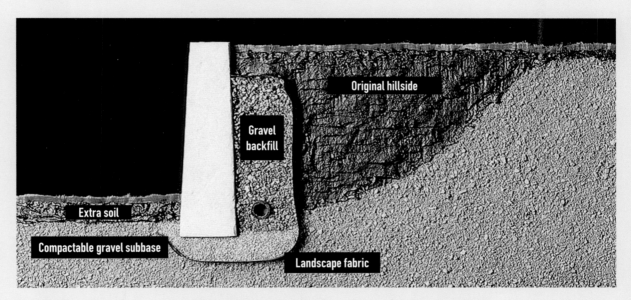

**(A) Increase the level** area above the wall by positioning the wall well forward from the top of the hill. Fill in behind the wall with extra soil, which is available from sand-and-gravel companies.

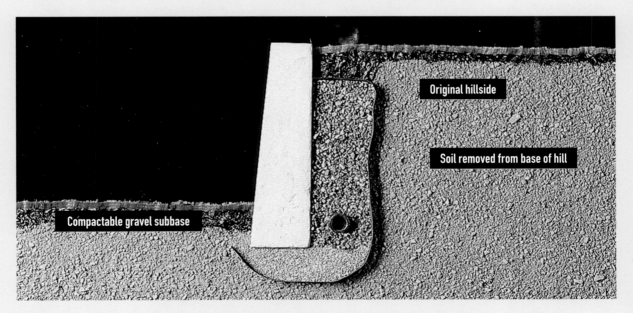

**(B) Keep the basic** shape of your yard by positioning the wall near the top of the hillside. Use the soil removed at the base of the hill to fill in near the top of the wall.

## Tips for Building Retaining Walls

Backfill with crushed stone and install a perforated drain pipe about 6" above the bottom of the backfill. Vent the pipe to the side or bottom of the retaining wall, where runoff water can flow away from the hillside without causing erosion.

Make a stepped trench when the ends of a retaining wall must blend into an existing hillside. Retaining walls are often designed so the ends curve or turn back into the slope.

**Overlapping flanges**

**Perforated Crushed stone backfill**

**Pins**

**Perforated drainpipe**

**Compactable gravel subbase**

**First row installed upside**

**Landscape fabric**

**Pins**

**Interlocking wall blocks** do not need mortar. Some types are held together with a system of overlapping flanges that automatically set the backward pitch (batter) as the blocks are stacked, as shown in this project. Other types of blocks use fiberglass pins (inset).

1   Excavate the hillside, if necessary. Allow 12" of space for crushed stone backfill between the back of the wall and the hillside. Use stakes to mark the front edge of the wall. Connect the stakes with mason's string, and use a line level to check for level.

2   Dig out the bottom of the excavation below ground level, so it is 6" lower than the height of the block. For example, if you use 6"-thick block, dig down 12". Measure down from the string in multiple spots to make sure the bottom base is level.

3   Line the excavation with strips of landscape fabric cut 3 ft. longer than the planned height of the wall. Make sure all seams overlap by at least 6".

4   Spread a 6" layer of compactable gravel over the bottom of the excavation as a subbase and pack it thoroughly. A rented tamping machine, or jumping jack, works better than a hand tamper for packing the subbase.

5   Lay the first course of block, aligning the front edges with the mason's string. (When using flanged block, place the first course upside down and backward.) Check frequently with a level and adjust, if necessary, by adding or removing subbase material below the blocks.

6   Lay the second course of block according to manufacturer's instructions, checking to make sure the blocks are level. (Lay flanged block with the flanges tight against the underlying course.) Add 3 to 4" of gravel behind the block, and pack it with a hand tamper.

7   Make half-blocks for the corners and ends of a wall, and use them to stagger vertical joints between courses. Score full blocks with a circular saw and masonry blade, then break the blocks along the scored line with a maul and chisel.

8   Add and tamp crushed stone, as needed, to create a slight downward pitch (about ¼" of height per foot of pipe) leading to the drain pipe outlet. Place the drain pipe on the crushed stone, 6" behind the wall, with the perforations face down. Make sure the pipe outlet is unobstructed. Lay courses of block until the wall is about 18" above ground level, staggering the vertical joints.

9   Fill behind the wall with crushed stone, and pack it thoroughly with the hand tamper. Lay the remaining courses of block, except for the cap row, backfilling with crushed stone and packing with the tamper as you go.

10   Before laying the cap block, fold the end of the landscape fabric over the crushed stone backfill. Add a thin layer of topsoil over the fabric, then pack it thoroughly with a hand tamper. Fold any excess landscape fabric back over the tamped soil.

11   Apply construction adhesive to the top course of block, then lay the cap block. Use topsoil to fill in behind the wall and to fill in the base at the front of the wall. Install sod or plants, as desired.

# Metric Conversions

## Metric Equivalent

| Inches (in.) | 1/64 | 1/32 | 1/25 | 1/16 | 1/8 | 1/4 | 3/8 | 2/5 | 1/2 | 5/8 | 3/4 | 7/8 | 1 | 2 | 3 | 4 | 5 | 6 | 7 | 8 | 9 | 10 | 11 | 12 | 36 | 39.4 |
|---|---|---|---|---|---|---|---|---|---|---|---|---|---|---|---|---|---|---|---|---|---|---|---|---|---|---|
| Feet (ft.) | | | | | | | | | | | | | | | | | | | | | | | | 1 | 3 | 3 1/12 |
| Yards (yd.) | | | | | | | | | | | | | | | | | | | | | | | | | 1 | 1 1/12 |
| Millimeters (mm) | 0.40 | 0.79 | 1 | 1.59 | 3.18 | 6.35 | 9.53 | 10 | 12.7 | 15.9 | 19.1 | 22.2 | 25.4 | 50.8 | 76.2 | 101.6 | 127 | 152 | 178 | 203 | 229 | 254 | 279 | 305 | 914 | 1,000 |
| Centimeters (cm) | | | | | | | 0.95 | 1 | 1.27 | 1.59 | 1.91 | 2.22 | 2.54 | 5.08 | 7.62 | 10.16 | 12.7 | 15.2 | 17.8 | 20.3 | 22.9 | 25.4 | 27.9 | 30.5 | 91.4 | 100 |
| Meters (m) | | | | | | | | | | | | | | | | | | | | | | | | .30 | .91 | 1.00 |

## Converting Measurements

| To Convert: | To: | Multiply by: |
|---|---|---|
| Inches | Millimeters | 25.4 |
| Inches | Centimeters | 2.54 |
| Feet | Meters | 0.305 |
| Yards | Meters | 0.914 |
| Miles | Kilometers | 1.609 |
| Square inches | Square centimeters | 6.45 |
| Square feet | Square meters | 0.093 |
| Square yards | Square meters | 0.836 |
| Cubic inches | Cubic centimeters | 16.4 |
| Cubic feet | Cubic meters | 0.0283 |
| Cubic yards | Cubic meters | 0.765 |
| Pints (U.S.) | Liters | 0.473 (Imp. 0.568) |
| Quarts (U.S.) | Liters | 0.946 (Imp. 1.136) |
| Gallons (U.S.) | Liters | 3.785 (Imp. 4.546) |
| Ounces | Grams | 28.4 |
| Pounds | Kilograms | 0.454 |
| Tons | Metric tons | 0.907 |

| To Convert: | To: | Multiply by: |
|---|---|---|
| Millimeters | Inches | 0.039 |
| Centimeters | Inches | 0.394 |
| Meters | Feet | 3.28 |
| Meters | Yards | 1.09 |
| Kilometers | Miles | 0.621 |
| Square centimeters | Square inches | 0.155 |
| Square meters | Square feet | 10.8 |
| Square meters | Square yards | 1.2 |
| Cubic centimeters | Cubic inches | 0.061 |
| Cubic meters | Cubic feet | 35.3 |
| Cubic meters | Cubic yards | 1.31 |
| Liters | Pints (U.S.) | 2.114 (Imp. 1.76) |
| Liters | Quarts (U.S.) | 1.057 (Imp. 0.88) |
| Liters | Gallons (U.S.) | 0.264 (Imp. 0.22) |
| Grams | Ounces | 0.035 |
| Kilograms | Pounds | 2.2 |
| Metric tons | Tons | 1.1 |

## Converting Temperatures

Convert degrees Fahrenheit (F) to degrees Celsius (C) by following this simple formula: Subtract 32 from the Fahrenheit temperature reading. Then mulitply that number by 5/9. For example, 77°F - 32 = 45. 45 × 5/9 = 25°C.

To convert degrees Celsius to degrees Fahrenheit, multiply the Celsius temperature reading by 9/5, then add 32. For example, 25°C × 9/5 = 45. 45 + 32 = 77°F.

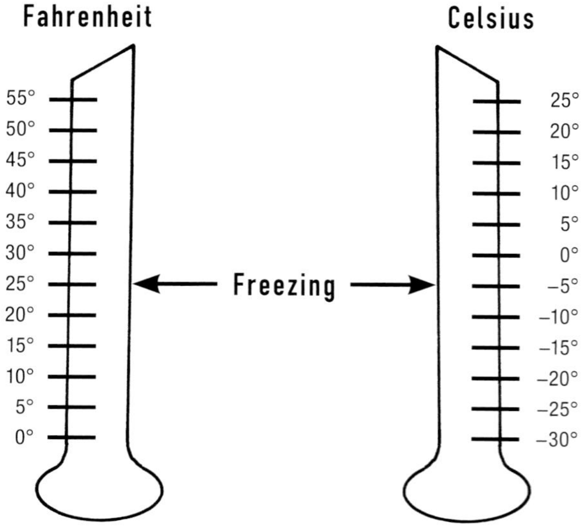

# Index

First published in 2013 by Cool Springs Press, an imprint of the Quayside Publishing Group, 400 First Avenue North, Suite 400, Minneapolis, MN 55401

Cool Springs Press titles are also available at discounts in bulk quantity for industrial or sales-promotional use. For details write to Special Sales Manager at Cool Springs Press, 400 First Avenue North, Suite 400, Minneapolis, MN 55401 USA. To find out more about our books, visit us online at www.coolspringspress.com.

Library of Congress Cataloging-in-Publication Data

HomeSkills. Landscaping : how to use plants, structures & surfaces to transform your yard.
    pages cm
  ISBN 978-1-59186-582-7 (softcover)
  1. Landscape construction.  I. Cool Springs Press. II. Title: Landscaping. III. Title: Home skills. Landscaping.

TH4961.H663 2013
712'.6--dc23

2013005625

Design Manager: Cindy Samargia Laun
Design and layout: Mary Rohl
Cover and series design: Carol Holtz

Printed in China
10 9 8 7 6 5 4 3 2 1

**NOTICE TO READERS**

*For safety, use caution, care, and good judgment when following the procedures described in this book. The publisher cannot assume responsibility for any damage to property or injury to persons as a result of misuse of the information provided.*

*The techniques shown in this book are general techniques for various applications. In some instances, additional techniques not shown in this book may be required. Always follow manufacturers' instructions included with products, since deviating from the directions may void warranties. The projects in this book vary widely as to skill levels required: some may not be appropriate for all do-it-yourselfers, and some may require professional help.*

*Consult your local building department for information on building permits, codes, and other laws as they apply to your project.*